HARD KNOCKS

HARD KNOCKS

Memoir of a Small Moment

Ray Lopez

FOREWORD BY
Paula Gill Lopez

RESOURCE *Publications* · Eugene, Oregon

HARD KNOCKS
Memoir of a Small Moment

Resource Publications
An Imprint of Wipf and Stock Publishers
199 W. 8th Ave., Suite 3
Eugene, OR 97401

www.wipfandstock.com

PAPERBACK ISBN: 978-1-7252-5917-1
HARDCOVER ISBN: 978-1-7252-5918-8
EBOOK ISBN: 978-1-7252-5919-5

Manufactured in the U.S.A.   JUNE 26, 2020

"For a small moment have I forsaken thee; but with great mercies will I gather thee. In a little wrath I hid my face from thee for a moment; but with everlasting kindness will I have mercy on thee, saith the LORD the Redeemer."

—Isaiah 54: 7, 8

"We proclaim to you what we have seen and heard, so that you also may have fellowship with us. And our fellowship is with the Father and with his son, Jesus Christ. We write this to make our joy complete."

—1 John 1: 3, 4

"Are you experienced? Have you ever been experienced? Well, I have."

—Jimi Hendrix

CONTENTS

PREVIOUSLY PUBLISHED POEMS

"The Rape" was first published in CQ California State Poetry Quarterly, Special Winter Issue 1985 Volume XII Number 4; Electrum THE QUARTERLY POETRY MAGAZINE, NO.38 SPRING 1986 and OCCIDENT U.C. Berkeley's Literary Magazine Vol. CIII, No. 1 1990

"The Twilight Zone" was originally published in the Fall 1984 issue of Joint Endeavor, a literary magazine previously edited and published by inmates at Huntsville State Penetentiary P.O. Box 32, Huntsville, Texas 77340

FOREWORD

I MET RAY LOPEZ WHEN I WAS 16. HE WAS 15. HE WAS TALL, DARK, and handsome. He wore overalls and black-rimmed glasses. His shoulders were broad and his reputation was bad. I was smitten.

I experienced Ray's reputation from a distance, while I experienced his heart up close. He was smart, charming, and funny. When he went down to Florida with his family to visit his grandparents one Christmas, he brought me back a tee shirt with a big red apple. It read, "I like you." Our daughter occasionally wears it today.

There was something about the class of 1977 at Commack HS North. The "hooligans" seemed to be the devil's spawn. They were puppets and the devil pulled the strings. Looking back, it was like they were cursed. So many in Ray's class ended up in prison or did not survive into their early twenties. When the class of '77 graduated, a twelve-foot chain link fence was erected around the perimeter of the school property. I always thought it wasn't so much to keep students in, but rather to keep the 1977 graduates out.

Just as God uses all things for good, the devil uses all things for evil. He stokes the rage of racism with alcohol and drugs and overcomes unconditional love with indifference and pride. Though I didn't know it at the time, there was a supernatural war going on during Ray's formative years—the prize was his soul. This is the account of that bloody battle. This memoir describes a young boy who seethed with fury, who descended into the depths of self-destructive self-loathing as a teenager, who was tormented and nourished by an illicit drug phase, followed by a Lithium/ Thorazine craze, and finally a Jimi Hendrix purple haze.

The Ray in this memoir is unrecognizable to me. Even though I "grew up" with him and have heard all the stories many times, the man into which he has evolved is such a powerful devotee of Christ that it's difficult to imagine him otherwise. His email address begins "raylohalo," a nickname he was christened with by a colleague in the U.S. Probation Office years ago. I need not say more. The only explanation for the transformation is Jesus.

I left college after two years and moved back to Commack an atheist. Those who believed in God, who relied upon God, were weak. I understood God to be a crutch for people who were unable to do for themselves. Ray's conversion paved the way for my own rebirth.

Today, I am a woman of strong faith. "The only thing that matters is faith expressing itself as love"—Galatians 5:6. My relationship with Jesus is my ALL. My first step on the road from atheist to Jesus freak began in 1980 with the realization that if Ray wasn't dead, there must be a God. I pray that by reading this book your faith is similarly awakened.

Paula Gill Lopez

ACKNOWLEDGMENTS

We had been at the Huntington Chapel in Shelton, Connecticut for a few months, and the prophet David Wagner was visiting the church for the first time in 2005. He came from Jubilee, a large church in Southern Florida, a man of average height with short dark black hair, dark brown eyes that looked deep, and a little pouch around the waist. After serving in the Baptist church for fifteen years, I knew how to share the Gospel and lead others to Christ. I knew I was an evangelist the moment I accepted the Lord through a baptism of the Holy Spirit. I knew nothing about the gift of prophecy but had read a lot about false prophets in the Bible. I was skeptical to say the least. The Body was moving in open corporate prayer, about one hundred brothers and sisters free in the Spirit to pray as one felt led. Powerful, passionate, some cried out, some prayed softly, some prayed in the Spirit in a language that was their own gift from God. It moved in waves at times rising to a crescendo of many voices, then crashing to the shore of a single voice. Pastor Doug preached on prophecy, a word of knowledge, in which God would reveal a piece of your past through one with a prophetic gift to bring healing, or a word of wisdom to reveal his plan for your future. David started pacing back and forth across the front of the church calling forward those who wanted to hear a word from the Lord. I knelt on my knees in the middle of the room, and I wasn't moving. I was good right there, where God had planted me, knowing He heard my prayers, the body heard my prayers, on my knees, eyes closed, rocking back and forth as the worship team played. I heard David moving through the body, praying and speaking words over people. He paused for a moment. People prayed and cried, "Thank you Jesus, Hallelujah, thank you Jesus, thank you Lord." I felt a hand on the top of my head, then David's voice, a subtle Southern drawl, but sharp in tone, "evangelist, evangelist, evangelist." I thought so what, big deal, he heard me pray. Anyone who heard my prayer would know I am an evangelist. I had been working as a federal probation officer since 1990 and often prayed for my cases, mobsters, gang members, addicts. Then God spoke through David, "You have been through the School of Hard Knocks," and I knew I was hearing the voice of God through this man. That refrain of my life, spoken by my earthly father, again and again. I fell down on my face. I knew it was real. God was speaking through this man. He spoke through David and said, "You will evangelize the hardcore, one at a time." My plan and vision as an evangelist was sharing my testimony in an auditorium filled with the lost who would all rush forward after hearing me speak to receive God's gift of salvation. God knew my prideful heart and called me out on it right there on the floor of the Huntington Chapel, and my life as an evangelist has been just as He said, the hardcore, a condition of the soul, one at a time. With the deepest gratitude within my mind and heart, I praise my Lord and Savior Jesus Christ for the sacrifice of his blood and breath. I thank my parents, Alfred and Mary Lopez, for their lives and their love. Dad taught me about the discipline of the mind, body, and eventually love. Mom never blinked, not even for a small moment. She looked me in the eyes and loved me enough to let me go in faith, love, and hope. I thank my Uncles, Ramon and George, for their invaluable assistance as family historians. The stories they shared helped clarify the narrative and brought my grandparents to life beyond my memories. I am blessed to be a second-generation son of Cuban, Mexican, and Spanish immigrants. Pop, my paternal grandfather, left us too soon but left an enduring legacy of strength. My paternal grandmother, Porfilia, was an intercessory prayer warrior who fought against evil and won daily victories. My maternal grandmother, Aurelia, was an independent woman who taught my Mom how to make her own way. And my Mom's dad, Benigño, loved me beyond time and reason. I thank my sister, Teresa, who always stayed close enough that I always felt her love. She either witnessed or lived through many of the stories in my memoir and brought to life some stories of her own that were lost in the dark corners of my mind. She saw the scratches on the wall! I thank my brothers, Steve and Pete, for their love and support and having the insight to learn from my youthful mistakes. They were also invaluable readers of this narrative. I thank all my English professors at Cal State Hayward and Cal (Don Marcos, Robert Pinsky, Gary Soto, and John Bishop) for their honesty and encouragement. I thank my brother in Christ, Vincent Carbone, for his careful reading of this book and sharing what God was saying to him about my story. I thank my copy editor, Rich Gelfand. We became friends through this journey. I thank all the Hooligans and friends and enemies who live on each day and some in our memories. I pray mercy and grace for Tony, John D., Brian R., Larry, and for the family and friends they left behind. I thank Brian B., Pat D., and Steve Deluca for their enduring friendship and direct input into the text. I thank my children, Tebben and Jesse, for their love, their support, and their invaluable input into this book. Finally, and second only to Christ in my life, I thank my beloved wife, Dr. Paula Gill Lopez, the strongest beacon of love in my life.

1

NO

"No"— MY FIRST WORD, THE REFRAIN OF MY CHILDHOOD, MY RE-
sponse to everything. Raymond, do you want some fruit? No. Do
you want something to drink? No. Do you want to go outside and
play? No. A negative child imbued with a predisposed anger nur-
tured by my circumstances, my family nicknamed me Groucho.
Mom disciplined me with the paddle and the wooden spoon. She
didn't trust me out of sight and put me on "time out" in the kitchen,
where I beat time by the rhythmic banging of the back of my head
against the wall. Tears became useless. The sympathy gained from
my mother disappeared when upon receiving an epiphany in par-
enting one day, she proclaimed, "Those tears won't work anymore,
and if you want to cry, I'll give you something to cry about."

It took nearly nineteen years of my life to see that God prepared a place for me. I just needed to find it and my real identity.
The journey began in my parents' kitchen. After being up for days
on booze and speed, anger, way above my normal base, overcame
me. I became furious, frustrated at what I don't know and exploded in a fury—smashing chairs, bashing appliances, and breaking
lights. My sister, Teresa, came in to see the tornado in the house
and screamed, "What are you doing!?" I ran out the front door,
and the telephone pole called to me; banging my head against it

seemed like the right thing to do at the time. Teresa followed me and jumped on my back, still screaming, "What are you doing?!" A fair question but it interfered with God's plan, so I threw her to the ground and continued down the street. Mom pulled up in her green Chrysler Cordova with Corinthian leather seats and said, "Raymond, get in the car," which I did. She began telling me about this place where I could go to rest and that she could take me there to rest; it sounded good. I needed to rest. I could see God's plan unfolding. And when I said yes, I heard the sound of my voice amplified throughout the Universe, and I knew I needed to go to this place, South Oaks Hospital. South Oaks. It sounded so nice, so peaceful. South Oaks.

My roots are buried in a spiritual dichotomy. My paternal grandparents were devout Roman Catholics and my grandmother, Porfilia Reyes, an intercessory prayer warrior, battled for my soul. Orphaned at the age of three, her godmother took her into her home in Lagos de Moreno in the Province of Jalisco, Mexico. Porfilia cared for her godmother's wealthy Patron, an elderly incapacitated man. Later, at eighteen, facing a difficult situation working as a maid for another family in Mexico City, Porfilia's godmother once again came to her aid and arranged for her to travel to New York City with a representative of the Bank of Mexico to work as the family's maid. Soon thereafter, she met my grandfather, Thomas Camba Lopez (Pop), an immigrant from Spain, via Cuba. They married and raised three sons: my Uncle Tom, the oldest; my father, Alfred; and the youngest, Ramon. They were Pop and Tita to their grandchildren.

A Latino machismo heritage exists on my Dad's side of the family. In the public eye, the father, the head of the family, ruled. But the mother, the *heart* of the family, really ran the show. Pop stood 5'2" tall with 140 pounds of ripped muscle packed onto his diminutive frame. My favorite story—a public display of machismo and family honor—involved a battle with the O'Rileys. Uncle Ramon fought one of the O'Riley boys about his age. He got the best of this lad, and the next oldest brother stepped in and forced Uncle Ramon to say "Uncle," thereby acknowledging his defeat.

Dad jumped in and beat up that kid, which prompted the next oldest brother to beat up Dad, which brought in Uncle Tom, who jumped on top of the kid who beat up Dad and pinned him to the ground. While this was happening, Mr. O'Riley came home from work, pulled Uncle Tom off his son and threw him to the sidewalk. Pop then came home from his job as a short order cook in time to see this assault and challenged Mr. O'Riley to fight, taking the traditional bare-knuckled boxer stance. O'Riley, 6'2" and 200 pounds, towered over Pop. Pop, a champion fighter in Spain, boxed his ears off. After his victory, word got around and Dad and his brothers never got challenged to another fight in Washington Heights. In the 1930s, their neighborhood was 95 percent Irish Catholic, with a few Italian, Hispanic, and Polish families. Pop worked hard, saved his money, and his family became the first on the block to own a car.

Dad and his brothers excelled in academics and athletics. Dad participated in competitive cycling from the time he was fifteen. He qualified to race in Salt Lake City for a spot on the U.S. Olympic Road Racing Team when he was eighteen and still in high school. Pop suffered a stroke around the same time and instead of the Olympics, Dad stayed home to work to help provide for the family. Tita also thought he was too young to go. In the 1970s, Pop died in church from a massive heart attack while serving as an usher. He was eighty years old. Porfilia lived to be a month shy of one hundred. She lived with us the last decade of her life. Porfilia prayed on her knees every day for an hour. She prayed for me during my dark years, and I survived. I didn't understand why but was always fascinated by her faith and drawn to her religion and cherished objects: her Bible, missal, and statues of the Virgin Mary, Christ, Saint Francis of Assisi, and others. I believed that she knew God.

> "This Woman Knows God"
> She lived
> close
> to a century.
> She loves

for an eternity.
She died
and I live
because she prayed for my soul.

She loved us
with her enchiladas,
Mexican pastries
and the egg in the bowl
she whipped with the rhythm
of her life
strong, steady
powerful like her faith.

It was then I knew,
as a child,
watching her whip the egg
with the suca,
listening to her sing
the old songs she learned
as an orphaned child
servant in the city.
The spoon
became a silver blur
in her hand
and was like her prayers,
strong, steady
powerful.
The egg was sweet
Yellow
warm like the Florida sun,
like her touch,
her songs
her prayers
it was then I knew
this woman knows God.

She gave me
one of my earliest lessons
on pride.
She spoke of her ancestry,
the Basque,

and her eyes,
the rich, reddish brown
color of her skin,
the features of her face
spoke of the Indian.

All these things
she gave to me
and all these things
slipped through my fingers.

I had to die
and be born again
to find these gifts
again,
to find that it is
just as she said.
And I find myself again,
in her cocina
watching her whip the egg
with the rhythm of her soul,
anticipating the sweet taste
on my tongue,
that I relish once more
as I tell my daughter
about mi Abuela
and delight in her joy
as her eyes fill with pride
my eyes fill with tears
as I proudly tell her
of mi Abuela's blood
the Basque,
the Indian,
this woman who knows God.

My maternal grandparents fled from Havana in the 1920s during the fascist rule of Batista. My grandmother, Aurelia, owned a beauty salon in Havana. She later opened a salon in New York City. She believed in spiritualism and sought truth through Tarot Card reading, opening the door for darkness to enter her life and the next two generations. Demonized, she often came under spells of rage, grabbed whatever kitchen tool or makeshift weapon she could find, and chased Mom and my Uncle George, like a wild banshee. Sometimes she caught them, and violent punishment followed for whatever indiscretion occurred—perceived or committed. She also lamented as one of the greatest hypochondriacs of her time. She was miserable, and I often wondered how she could be so sick all the time, yet look so healthy. She was a sturdy woman who helped me appreciate my own good health. My grandfather, Benigño Roqueñi, a deist who rejected all forms of religion, worshipped women and scotch whiskey. All who knew him loved his kind and gentle manner. We called them Tita and Tito. They made up part of an inseparable trinity. They traveled from Cuba to New York with Tito's best friend, Ernesto Rutherford, know to us a Padrino, my mother's godfather. They all retired in Miami, and lived within walking distance of each other. Padrino, a heavy-drinking, heavy-smoking Merchant Marine cook, whose wife left him while he was out at sea, had a deep, gravelly voice with a heavy Spanish accent. He loved reading cheap Spanish western novels, was a Florida state dominoes champion, and looked like Humphrey Bogart.

My paternal grandmother, Porfilia Lopez Reyes,
was an intercessory prayer warrior.

Pop, Tita and the boys, Uncle Tom on the left, Ramon on Pop's lap
and Dad on the right.

Mom with her parents and her brother George.

And so, looking back upon generations, the stage was set for the battle over my soul clashing darkness and light which, in their outer limits, occupy the same space as the beginning of one signals the end of the other. It starts with a single step in one direction or another.

"One generation shall commend your works to another, and shall declare your mighty acts."

PSALM 145:4

2

BABY STEPS

A CAULDRON OF PREJUDICE BECAME AN INCUBATOR FOR MY AN-
ger, which grew into adolescent rage. I was born on September
1, 1959, at Bethany Deaconess Hospital in the Bushwick section
of Brooklyn, the second of four children born through the marriage of Mary and Alfred Lopez. My parents came from the same
neighborhood in Washington Heights, New York. Separated by
four years, they met when Dad became Mom's piano teacher. They
began their relationship as young adults, and Dad romanced Mom
through passionate love letters, written while in the Air Force
serving in the Philippines during the Korean War. They married
shortly after he returned. My parents, my older sister, Teresa, and
I lived in a cold water flat on Bushwick Avenue. One month after
my birth, we moved to Suffolk County, Long Island, specifically
Commack, with a population of about 30,000—95 percent white,
Irish, Italian, Jewish, and Roman Catholic. Only a handful of Black
and Hispanic families lived in Commack.

By the time we moved to Long Island, my paternal grandparents had relocated to Miami. When I was eleven months old,
we drove down south to visit them in a black Volkswagen Beetle,
with me and Teresa precariously settled on the back seat. We drove
straight through a hurricane. Upon arrival, inspired by being

cramped up for twenty-six hours, I stepped out of the car and took my first steps. Thus began our yearly trip to Miami, and three years later, on such a trip, I find my earliest memory poetically rooted in a historically significant event in American history.

We normally traveled to Miami for summer vacations, but on this trip, we visited for Thanksgiving. My parents always took turns at the wheel and drove straight through, usually taking up to thirty hours. This time, however, we stopped at a hotel in Georgia. My younger brother, Steve, had joined the family, making us five. After we settled into our room, I saw Mom sitting in front of the TV sobbing. I asked Dad why, and he told me President Kennedy died. "Who's President Kennedy?" I asked, and he explained, "He's like the king of our country." Now I knew a bit about kings and queens and knights and dragons, and I immediately became concerned that our trip could not continue. I believed that the king drove the first car in line on the road and without him, there would be no one to lead us; we'd have to turn back. That day, I learned otherwise. Dad must've been powerfully affected as well because when we headed back out to the highway, he sideswiped a telephone pole, which startled us because of his typically amazing driving skills—second only to President Kennedy. Another of my earliest memories is from the South a few years later. When at a rest stop, faced with a pair of water fountains displaying signs saying "Colored" and "White," I drank from the "Colored" fountain ... and nobody seemed to notice.

Before they moved to Miami, my siblings and I each took turns staying with Tito and Tita in their apartment in Washington Heights. Tito made the best Cuban sandwiches, and there was a candy store right outside the building where he would take me to buy candy and monster magazines. I loved all the old Universal horror films. From my earliest cinematic awakening, I loved *Dracula*, *Frankenstein*, *The Mummy*, and *The Wolfman*, who frightened me the most. With *Dracula*, if you wore a necklace of garlic, a cross, and carried a vial of Holy Water (which you could steal from the church), you'd be safe. I could easily outrun the *Frankenstein* monster and *The Mummy*. But *The Wolfman* could run like Jesse Owens. *The Wolfman* scared me. *The Wolfman* could catch me.

Tito worked as a bellman and could've been a hotel manager. Several times over the years the position became available, but he never applied. He worked as the acting manager until they filled the position, then stepped down and returned to be the bell captain in charge of all the bellmen. When he started working there it was named The Abbey Hotel. The Abbey catered to visitors from Central and South America. Tito, Spanish-speaking and suave, possessed a phenomenal memory for names and became very popular. All four of my grandparents became friends, and Tito helped Pop get a job as the hotel timekeeper. Pop, sitting and smiling at his desk at the employee entrance, greeted and registered the arrival and departure of all employees. One summer during his high school years, my Uncle George got to work at the hotel and see his father in action. Everyone loved and respected Tito. When guests reappeared for a new stay, he always remembered their names, family history, and even the chronology of their children. He amazed them.

Regardless, George felt ashamed of his father for being just a bellman and one day had the temerity to ask him why. Tito explained that the hotel manager worked six days a week; he only worked five and made more money because of his tips. He managed money well, and others considered my mom and uncle to be the rich kids on the block. They owned the first telephone in the building and welcomed the neighbors to use it. They also enjoyed the first washing machine, located in the kitchen, and the first black-and-white TV set, featuring a five-inch screen. They later became the first family in the building to own a color TV. Tita's beauty salon, Marietta's, served numerous clients, and between bouffants and hotel tips they did very well, even being able to afford a housekeeper. Tito, Tita, and Padrino moved to Little Havana, Miami, in the '70s.

I loved going to Miami. Both sets of grandparents lived there, as well as my Uncle Tom, Aunt Joan, and older cousins Tommy and KC. We numbered six: Teresa, 15 months older than me, my younger brothers Steve and Pete, and my parents. We'd pile in the Chrysler Town & Country station wagon with wood siding. As we got older, Teresa claimed the back seat to herself for sleeping, and the boys slept in the back with the rear-facing seat folded down so we could stretch out. We counted how many different state plates we saw, but the biggest highlight was seeing the first signs for South of the Border, which started in North Carolina about one hundred miles away from our destination and reappeared every ten or so miles. I loved the fried shrimp at the Big Boy restaurant and the Indian Trading Post where our parents bought us souvenirs. When we drove through Georgia, we called the oak/cypress trees, with Spanish moss hanging down from the big branches, "Gitche Gumee trees." They spooked us at night. Florida appeared as another planet to me, with alligators, palm trees, coconuts, sharp grass, and supersized insects.

Pop had a profound effect on me and provided the impetus for years of bodybuilding and powerlifting that have literally and figuratively shaped my life. We stayed at Pop and Porfilia's house, as there was plenty of room. After we arrived, Pop would come around from the backyard, where he could often be found chopping down sugar cane with his machete; muscular brown arms, veins popping, sweating through his bandana. He always raised my extremely skinny arms, squeezed the place where my biceps were supposed to be, and proclaimed, "Mantequilla." I would watch as he chopped down the sugar cane growing in the backyard then suck the sweetest taste from the stalk of cane he offered. I loved the backyard, an exotic jungle of banana, grapefruit, mango trees and birdbaths, all surrounding a concrete shrine to the Virgin Mary. Tita, a short, sturdy Mexican-Indian woman with dark hair and almond eyes, constantly said "magnificent" to describe the quality of anything created by her grandchildren. Manual labor had grown muscles in Pop's arms, and there was warmth and safety to be found in Tita's arms, where she loved you with her tamales, enchiladas, flan, and Mexican pastries. She looked Native American but only spoke proudly of her Basque ancestry, not her Indian roots.

Mom's parents lived in an apartment in Little Havana. We would stick to the plastic coverings over the furniture and would literally have to peel ourselves from the clutching couch to escape into the Florida sun. My Mom inherited Tita's passion for preserving cleanliness. Padrino lived down the street. He taught us how to catch chameleons by making a noose at the end of a long blade of grass and slipping it around the lizard's neck if you were still enough, held your breath and could keep your hand steady. We sat in his smoky kitchen while he cooked, and we enjoyed steak and French fry omelets for breakfast and chicharrones de carnitas for snacks. Padrino, the master of roasted pork, started that process with a trip to the local pig farm. It was a right-of-passage machismo event, but my sister Teresa insisted on going because she was twelve and the oldest grandchild. So all the kids joined Tito, Padrino, and Dad on this particular journey. The pig probably weighed 200 pounds, but the two muscular brown-skinned teenagers lifted it, quite easily, by tying the front legs with thick rope and hoisting the pig up with a harness. The high-pitched squealing stunned us at first. We were amazed that such a large animal could make this ear-piercing noise. But we were given no warning of the slaughter to come. Standing only a few feet away, we felt the warmth of the beast's blood that splattered onto our faces as a young boy, no older than Teresa, plunged his knife deep just below the pig's neck. Blood flowed out in a rush, like a small wave, while he ripped the animal open, pulling his knife down the length of the body. The blood pooled in the dirt and splashed a bit as the organs were pulled out in the gutting—our baptism by blood. Teresa started crying and kept talking about how cute it was. I didn't see the pig again until we were back at Padrino's. Both sides of the family came together and joined in the preparation. The men dug a shallow hole in the ground, placed stones in it and built a tremendous fire with the wood Steve and I carried from the stack in the corner of the yard. The rod that hung over the pit, braced between two thick steel poles, had always been a mystery to me. I suddenly needed to piss very badly, ran into the house and into the bathroom, where I found the pig, laying in the bathtub partially covered with ice, staring at me. I pissed in my pants.

The huge fire sparked as the blood and oil dripped off the pig. It was still staring at me, but I looked away when Dad started playing his guitar and Uncle Tom joined him in a chorus of *Rancho Grande*. I loved when Uncle Tom broke into his Mexican yodeling and watched the sparks rise into the stars.

My cultural confusion during childhood took root in The American Dream. The theme of the great mixing bowl of cultures and ethnicities strived to make a big salad of totality where the individual flavors were blended together and tasted delicious, especially in suburbia. Through this fallacy, language—and to some extent, food and music—were lost in pursuit of assimilation. My bilingual parents learned Spanish at home and English at school, but in our home they only spoke Spanish as a secret language used to discuss things they didn't want us to understand. This mystified and confused me and added to my daily dosage of the differences between myself and others. Those differences became amplified, yet lovingly tempered, by visits to my grandparents' homes, where we melted into the smells and sounds of Cuba and Mexico.

"So whether you eat or drink or whatever you do, do it all for the glory of God."

1 CORINTHIANS 10:31

3

SCHOOL DAYS

MY PARENTS RAISED US ROMAN CATHOLIC, CONTINUING THE RE-
ligious tradition of my paternal grandparents. We received all
the sacraments and attended Catholic school and weekly Mass
at Christ the King. To compound the daily assault of insults and
racial slurs received from my classmates, Sister Mary Assault and
Battery educated us while Falling Down Father Foley offered no
absolution through confession. The smell of scotch whiskey, always strong in the confessional, led to the sound of deep snor-
ing, signaling the father's afternoon slumber and confession's end.
Being released from sin without paying any penance through
the repetitive recitation of one hundred "Our Fathers" offered a
special blessing. A few years later, Father Foley expelled me from
the confessional, (an experience I share with my sister), thereby
launching the future of my soul into limbo, after I began with the
requisite "Bless me Father for I have sinned," and confessed that "It
has been over a year since my last confession." I think Father Foley
believed that if you didn't confess once a week, your soul was lost
for eternity.

When I started school, I learned that I was different, that my
skin was darker, that I was a nigger, a spic, a Hershey Bar. My classmates reminded me every day, and I grew to be angry and angrier.

I fought each day, always outnumbered, alone, and on my own. My older sister tried to protect me when she could but had her own battles to fight. My classmates targeted every aspect of my being. And I smelled, literally, as Mom made me sardine sandwiches for lunch. By the time I got on the morning school bus, the oil oozed through the plastic baggie (pre-ziplock era) onto the brown paper lunch bag. The playground and battleground on the church parking lot consisted of hard asphalt pavement marked by several light poles. The main game, Keep Away, was also known as Kill the Man with the Ball. It involved the player in possession of the Spalding red rubber ball avoiding the pursuit of every other player intent upon pounding the ball carrier to the ground, piling on top and ripping the ball from his hands. Fortunately, I was the fastest kid in school. I had natural speed, enhanced by the need to escape my tormentors. My fleetness of foot frustrated my haters, which added to their fury after capturing me. One needed allies to be successful at this game. I was alone, always on my own.

I learned to take full advantage of any opportunity to connect. I knew that people appreciated speed and related to the story of Jesse Owens' success in the Olympics, where he defeated Hitler and the Nazis by winning four gold medals. So I tried out for the CYO track team. Tryouts took place on the same parking lot. The runners lined up and took off. I quickly gained a ten-yard lead on the others, who all passed me as I stopped dead at the finish line. I didn't know enough to cross the line. I joined the team, ran all the sprints, and anchored the relay team. I usually received the baton far behind our competitors but always caught up and passed them. I always crossed the finish line first to the resounding joy of the parents and grateful acknowledgment of my classmates, usually by a slight head nod. Speed gave me an advantage and tempered my torment.

There were hall monitors at Christ the King, trusted students positioned at the entrances/exits to the school building, which connected to the church. They prevented unauthorized entrance and escorted those in need of using the bathroom during recess. They constantly denied me entry while trying to evade my pursuers, and no sanctuary could be found in the locked church. Consequently, I made sure to relieve myself prior to recess, but it wasn't fail-safe. One day, suffering from a stomachache with my bowels about to burst, the guardians denied me access. They looked stunned as I stood before them while the brown ooze flowed from the bottom of my pants onto my shoes and the pavement. Then they laughed. My mother came to pick me up that day. My tormentors, further inspired by this unfortunate event, added new insults to their arsenal. But worse than that, after seeing the look of disappointment on Mom's face, I *felt* like shit, less than shit.

"...be quick to listen, slow to speak and slow to become angry. Because human anger does not bring about the righteousness that God desires."

JAMES 1: 19, 20

4

AM I A MAN OR A MOUSE?

THE KIDS ACTED SOMEWHAT KINDER IN MY NEIGHBORHOOD, BUT
I still fought often. One day, Tommy, Francis, and I played on
the driveway in front of my house. Tommy punched me in the
face, for a reason lost in time, and I landed on my ass. Shocked, I
responded by jumping up and running into the house. I felt sick
and cowardly, watching them from my bedroom window laughing as they walked over to Tommy's house. I thought of the Tom
& Jerry cartoon I watched that morning: Tom, sick and tired of
being pushed around by a big, burly beach bully cat, pondered his
dilemma, thinking to himself, "Am I a man or a mouse? Am I a
man or a mouse?" And I started asking myself, am I a man or a
mouse? I knew Tom, a cat, wasn't a mouse but acted like a man,
and I decided right then: I am a man. I marched over to Tommy's
house, pounded on the door and demanded that he come out and
fight me. He and Fran came out; Tommy and I began to wrestle,
but I quickly got him in a strong headlock and forced him to say
"uncle" three times before I let him go. But he fought dirty. The
minute I released him, he tried to jump me in violation of the long-
standing "uncle" code. He charged and I got him in a double leg
hold and slammed him to the ground. That finished it. Everyone
on the block knew I could fight.

Dad, a highly functional alcoholic, knew how to party, and my parents loved to invite the neighbors over for their weekly cocktail shindigs. Dad played the piano and guitar; it evolved into a regular hootenanny! These relationships led to acceptance from the kids on the block and a relatively normal experience of playing baseball, football, and basketball in someone's yard or down the street at Long Acres Elementary School. Unfortunately, my status as a chronic bedwetter—and the accompanying taunts—persisted. Perhaps my problems at school led to this condition, but Mom's frustrated response exacerbated the situation, as she hung the wet sheets outside to dry from my bedroom window. Each day the white flag flew, reminding all in the neighborhood that I wet the bed like a baby. Mom did her best to help me overcome this problem, but her efforts just led to a loss of sleep. At some point she purchased the Wee Alert, a wire mesh screen placed under the sheet and wired to an alarm. When moisture contacted it, a shrill alarm shocked me awake, theoretically, to prompt me to stop the urinary flow and successfully make it to the toilet on time. The opposite effect rendered me shocked, frightened, and peeing. It scared the shit out of me—literally, a number of times—sending me off to school in a state of fatigue as a companion to my building rage. It's amazing I was never electrocuted.

I also struggled with a serious lisp during my grade school years. I saw a speech therapist in school but continued lisping. Ultimately, someone, I'm thinking an orthodontist, devised a piece of metal to insert in my mouth with sharp, jagged points facing inward. When I attempted to speak, my tongue would press against the points, causing significant pain. This was supposed to train me to keep my tongue in the back of my mouth when talking. I wore it all day, and not only could I not pronounce words properly, but my tongue would bleed all the time. Between the Wee Alert and the jagged metal in my mouth, I was wired with a double whammy of being a lisping bed wetter. I only wore the mouth metal for a short time and just lost the lisp at some point.

But Mom, my biggest fan and lifesaver, went to every track meet, baseball game, and football game—sunshine, rain, or snow.

I could always see her and hear her shout words of encouragement, "Come on Raymond!" and a celebratory "Atta' Way!" when I succeeded. This tough woman used her strength to teach me many things, like riding a bike.

"Learning to Ride"
The sun was young—
and sparkled in the beads of sweat
that rolled down her neck,
as she turned the screwdriver,
and stripped off the training wheels.

Holding the alien bike
She slowly turned, her dark beautiful face,
Revealing a strange new smile.

"Come on Raymond.
It'll be fun.
Just peddle.
I'll hold you up."

Mounted on the familiar seat,
which never seemed so far from the ground,
I gazed down the driveway,
squirming, searching for the right position,
until I felt her palm
press against my bottom and my mounting panic
disappeared.
I turned and saw her,
radiant and ready.

Before I could think, we were off,
down the driveway
on the street
passing oak trees and parked cars
creating a breeze that blew sweat away!
I heard my heart
like it was in the air, pushing me.

"Peddle, Raymond, peddle!"
She laughed as I turned to see her running,
feet beating the street,
right arm swinging with the sound,

her left, a solid limb
with veins running red
that rushed to fill the edges of her cheeks.

My legs played catch up with the speed
until she took her hand
away
and they quit,
no balance
the street rose and scraped my knee!
Her voice pierced the pain
and my screaming,
"Raymond!
Look what you've done to your pants!"

And so it went.
The sun cooled
and after many turns, I gained some balance
with ripped dungarees and bloody knees.

Each time I picked the bike up
I understood through her eyes
the extent of her plan.
She had laughed long ago
and lost concern for my pants.
The sun was going down.

She left me
leaning on the curb;
ran into the house
and emerged
with the wooden spoon.

Running behind me,
Spoon slicing the air,
then her distant laughter
and the breeze

Mom and Dad

"Near the cross of Jesus stood his mother."

JOHN 19:25.

5

ALCOHOL

I STARTED DRINKING WHEN I WAS NINE AND BECAME AN ALCO-
holic by the age of ten. Not full blown of course; it takes a long time
to drink into that state of mind and body where every thought,
every small moment, is fueled by thirsty neurotransmitters, which
once resolved, even with only a thought, a plan, brings relief and
sometimes joy. Simple modeling. My parents' liquor cabinet held a
full stock, and Rheingold beer was abundant. The company spon-
sored the German Bicycle Sports Club, of which my dad raced as
the only minority member. He knew how to get along with people
and almost never lost his temper. During summer parties in the
back yard, I studied the men who gathered around a garbage can
full of beer and ice. They would chug down beers and become
happier and louder. As the evening wore on, they would retreat
into lounge chairs, drink cocktails, smoke cigarettes and cigars.
Then I'd make my move, slowly toward the can, then swiftly grab
as many beers as I could, slip to the side of the house and chug
them down as fast as I could, copying the men. I didn't get sick.
I felt the effect the very first time and loved it. It made me happy,
just like my parents when they drank. It helped me forget about my
troubles at school.

My childhood alcohol consumption personal best occurred at a sports club party at the club president's home. An unguarded fridge in the kitchen, filled with Rheingold, called to me. It provided easy access. As I already learned, the key to success as a childhood drinker . . . timing. One waited until the adults became drunk before making a move. I drank nine beers that day. No one noticed, and I didn't get sick, although I felt a little queasy on the ride home.

"Do not get drunk on wine which leads to debauchery."

EPHESIANS 5:18

6

VIETNAM

1968 IMPACTED MY PSYCHE ENORMOUSLY. I WAS IN THIRD GRADE,
and I learned about Vietnam from TV and a music lesson at school.

"Mothra"

I had all kinds of soldiers.
Japs were beige, Germans gray.
And I had Indians all different colors
and Cowboys and Saxons and Knights.
And I had Godzilla.
I'd set them up in front of the TV
for the six o'clock news
and wait for the Vietnam show.
When it started the battle began.
Some soldiers charged each other.
A German got stabbed by a Jap.
Others fired guns and threw grenades.
An American got blown up.
The Indians shot their arrows.
Down went a Cowboy, down a German
down an American, wrestling a Knight.
Then a TV soldier got wounded.
Blood squirted from his shoulder
and a bandage covered half his face.
They carried him off the screen on a stretcher.

Those were the times I'd call in Godzilla.
Calling Godzilla. Calling Godzilla.
I'd bring in the monster, mow everyone down,
raise him to my eye
and stomp the soldiers on the screen.
But he couldn't stop them.
Once I thought maybe Mothra could.
Calling Mothra.
Calling Mothra.
Help us Mothra

During Mr. Art's music lesson in the church basement, I learned about the war in Vietnam. He sweated constantly, causing the ceiling lights to reflect off his bald white head. He played the piano, and his supernatural hearing enabled him to hear what could not be heard. In a room of kids, he could hear the silence of someone not singing the song.

"Music Lesson on the Vietnam War"

There were about one hundred of us,
first, second, and third graders,
wearing our uniforms,
the girls in their brown, green, and maroon plaid dresses
and the boys in white shirts with maroon ties.
We sat on cold, metal fold-up chairs in the church basement,
where we ate lunch during the week
and received Communion on Sundays.
That day we had weekly music hour with Mr. Art
and could see the lights shining off his bald white head
as he pounded out the march on his piano,
"When Johnny comes marching home again hurrah, hurrah. . ."
But we couldn't get through the song
because he would stop and glare at us in silence
if someone wasn't singing.
We would stop, and start
"When Johnny comes marching home again hurrah, hurrah. . ."
and stop, and start
"When Johnny comes marching home again hurrah, hurrah. . ."
And each time Mr. Art would pound his piano harder;
and we would sing louder and louder until we were screaming

"WHEN JOHNNY COMES MARCHING HOME AGAIN
HURRAH, HURRAH!"
Until finally he stopped, stood up and walked over to us.
He pointed his yardstick, like an extension of his arm,
reaching out six feet or so
almost touching Patti, the cutest blonde-haired, pony-tailed,
blue-eyed girl.
"Why are you not singing young lady? Is there something wrong
with your voice?"
He loomed over her, lowering his stick as she stared at the floor.
Either he didn't notice or didn't care but she was sobbing softly.
"Look at me when I speak to you!"
She jumped up, now bawling out loud,
her face burning red,
she turned to run, but tripped over her chair,
crashing with it into our row behind her.
Her cheek brushed my leg,
leaving a wet spot.
She raced up the stairs, the sound of her cries echoing down.
In the stillness Mr. Art stood, framed in eternal stupidity.
Then a wave of whispering spread through the room
like dominoes falling in line, finally reaching my ear,
"Her brother Johnny was killed in Vietnam."

Years later, I watched the news broadcast of the Fall of Saigon
on August 9, 1974, and watched the last Americans being airlifted
in a helicopter. I thought about Patti's brother Johnny.

1969 inspired me. In the fourth grade, I got glasses and mar-
veled at the miracle of enhanced vision. The Mets won the World
Series, the Jets won the Super Bowl, and the Knicks won the NBA
Championship. The Universe stood in order, as far as my teams
were concerned. Playing and watching sports offered an escape
through which I could be somewhat accepted because of my speed,
agility, and athleticism.

My problems at school increased and intensified. I started
stealing from my classmates in retaliation for all the abuse. One
day, I stole a student's Batman cards, which we were allowed to
keep in our desks. Kids spent recess trading cards, and when these
were discovered missing, they convicted me without a proper

investigation and trial. Several kids surrounded me and tackled me to the ground. As always, I fought and wrestled vigorously, but when finally pinned to the asphalt, the cards were discovered in my pockets. The gang lifted me up, a kid on each limb, and carried me into the school building. The hall monitors happily granted us access. They took me directly to Sister Mary Beth's classroom, where she sat quietly, reading her Bible. She accepted the offering, affirmed the conviction, and wrote a letter to my parents documenting my crime. There would be many more letters sent home.

When the nuns escorted their classes to the cafeteria for lunch, I developed a habit of walking like a toy soldier in *March of the Wooden Soldiers*. It seemed like a good idea at the time as we walked in two straight lines, separated by gender. Lonely at lunch, I often sat by myself with my sardine sandwiches. They smelled, but I liked them, especially with the oil-soaked bread. I don't know who invented this delicacy, but I suspect it came through my grandparents and The Great Depression. The nuns got a break from their students during lunch. The kitchen staff and the priests monitored the cafeteria, making it much easier to get a hall pass for the bathroom. In class, you often had to wait until the lesson was over. Sometimes several students could be found squirming and suffering in their chairs. I guess the nuns didn't understand that urinary pain could impair a student's ability to learn. On this day, I was perfecting my wooden soldier march, free to swing my arms front and back, walking from the cafeteria, unescorted but in possession of my hall pass. Oblivious to the shrouded figure of Sister Mary Beth quickly approaching me on the same side of the hallway, our paths crossed. My right hand swung forward and smacked her vagina. She stopped, eyes burning, cheeks raging red, said nothing and slapped me across the face. She kept me from falling by grabbing my ear and dragging me down the hall to Vice Principal Sister Mary Kenneth's office. They sent another letter home. I kept the secret of how touching her there excited me. I had recently discovered masturbation, inspired by the artistic black and white nude photos published in Life Magazine. Sister Mary Beth was very pretty. I figured that masturbation was a sin and always felt guilty about it. I washed my hands sometimes thirty or forty times a day, causing my dry skin to crack and bleed, like the wounds of Christ, I figured. Warts grew on my hands during high school, more punishment for my sins, like the Biblical boils suffered by Job. Compound W didn't work, nor did tearing them out; they just grew back. Soap and water eventually washed my warts away when I worked a dishwasher at Mt. Fuji's Steakhouse while in high school.

Toward the end of fourth grade, my athletic ability inspired Sister Mary Kenneth to write another letter to my parents. During a free study time, I stood at the back of the classroom looking up a word in Webster's Dictionary. One of my tormentors, Richard, stood on the other side of the room, demanding that I give him the dictionary. He believed in the broken record technique and kept saying "Give me the dictionary." His persistence distracted me and drew my attention to his buckteeth chattering away, his pale complexion and bowl-cut black hair. After countless requests, I complied and launched the book across the classroom. A perfect throw, generating great speed and trajectory, it struck Richard right between the eyes, releasing a large amount of blood and cries.

Phones weren't needed in the classrooms, as the nuns communicated telepathically. Sister Mary Beth pointed toward the door; it was all she had to do when sending a child to the vice principal's office. The school building consisted of two stories with a single hallway. Grades one through four were on the first floor, with the fourth-grade classes at the end of the hall, farthest away from Sister Kenneth's office. As I stepped out, I saw motion at the end. Sister Kenneth was known to meditate and stare down the hall, ready to respond to the slightest movement. I started the long walk, focused on the black and white of her habit as she stood in her doorway waiting for me. At first she looked tiny. It felt like walking under water, my legs slow and heavy. But I kept going, and her silhouette grew larger and larger, slowly, until there she stood towering over me. No questions asked. She knew what I had done; why I had come. I didn't see the roundhouse slap coming from her right hand. I would've fallen over backward, but she supported my weight by grabbing the back of my neck with her left, while winding up to slap me again. She kept her nails long for such discipline, and as I jerked my head back to avoid the second blow, she pulled me forward, slightly losing her grip, causing a nail to break the first layer of skin halfway around my neck, nearly decapitating me! She also ripped out the stiches on the back of my head when she dragged me into her office by my left ear. The previous weekend we were visiting friends who lived nearby. They lived near a playground with a swing. I swung violently, higher and higher, higher than anyone else, getting ready to jump, oblivious to the rusted chain links that snapped at the peak, dumping me on the back of my head, opening a two-inch gash behind my left ear, knocking me out. I woke up in Mom's arms as she finished placing a bandage over the wound. The head injury traumatized me, but the visit to Dr. D. left a deeper scar. He had a home office and advised that he couldn't use any anesthesia because of my age and the head injury. When I flinched because of the pain, he slapped me and told me not to move again while he stitched me up.

I also sliced open my wrist in the church basement one night, breaking free from my imprisonment. It happened during a Valentine's Day dance for the parishioners. My parents volunteered me to hang coats with a couple of boys in the fifth grade. I didn't know them, and at first, they acted nice. But once the evening wore on, they thought it amusing to shove me into the phone closet while the music was playing. Initially, I played along with their joke, but when they refused to release me, I started banging on the heavy wooden door with my right fist. They laughed as I pounded harder and harder, and they kept laughing until my fist smashed through the thick, glass window at the top half of the door. My tormentors ran to get help, and I could see the white tendons exposed as my wrist opened and blood poured out. Some men came and carried me into the kitchen. They laid me down on a steel food prep table, and someone approached me with a dirty rag from the sink, but Mom appeared just in time to save me from the risk of infection. She stopped the bleeding, dressed my wound with a clean bandage and Dad carried me out of the church. I received several stitches (this time not from Dr. D.) and a long-lasting scar.

We continued attending Sunday Mass. During one such folk music service in the basement, I experienced a catatonic seizure. I couldn't move or speak. An unknown heaviness came upon my body; evil seized me. Dad carried me out of the church, but by the time we got home, I felt fine.

"The thief comes only to steal and kill and destroy."

JOHN 10:10

7

STRANGER DANGER

Dad's strength was surpassed only by his intelligence. I first felt his physical strength when he gave me and my siblings piggyback rides, all of us together. It took greater effort as we grew older, and he sometimes sweated through his white, sleeveless tee shirt. And as we got older, he grew stronger. The rides happened after dinner, after which he would head off to Manhattan College, where he earned his master's degree in electrical engineering. He became a top electronic engineer with over 50 patents, dozens of publications, and the highest recognition in the field. There is an antenna at Newark Airport that bears his name. Dad also trained for bicycle races year-round. During the winters, he rode the rollers in his workshop in the basement. This piece of equipment consisted of two large wooden pins for both wheels and required speed and balance to use. It generated a loud spinning noise that could be heard throughout the house. He trained every day and competed in races, sometimes around a velodrome track and sometimes on the road. Always a family event followed by a party, races offered another opportunity to get drunk. During one road race in Central Park, some thugs strung wire across the street to knock riders down and steal their bikes. They consequently stopped the race.

I had already learned there was danger in the world, and it could come at you anywhere, anytime.

On Halloween of that year, I engaged in some early trick-or-treating alone before dinner. All the other kids must've been having an early dinner, because I traveled alone on the block. I started on one side of the street, walked about a quarter mile to the end, then crossed over and started heading back home. Very few people answered the door. I guess they weren't ready or didn't want to disturb their meal. As I got near Long Acres, halfway home, a man drove by in the opposite direction. He was in a white Dodge Dart. He had black hair, black-rimmed glasses, and a big black mustache. It looked like a disguise. He drove very slowly, turned around, and started following me about ten feet behind. I knew he was after me and I had to run. As I took off, he hit the gas and accelerated. I cut through someone's backyard and climbed the ten-foot fence to get to the front of the school. The man knew the area because he pulled into the school parking lot the moment I hit the ground and started speeding toward me. I ran around the back of the building and started running to the other end. A twelve-foot space stretched between the building and another fence that lined the cornfield adjacent to the school. He whipped around the corner and continued to chase me. I jumped the fence and hid in the cornfield. I heard him stop and open his car door. He stood only a few feet away; I prayed he didn't hear me breathing. He returned to his car and drove around the neighborhood looking for me. I needed to get home . . . fast. I never thought to go to someone's house and ask for help. I just hid in bushes and ran through back-yards, making my way back, all the while watching him driving around slowly, looking for me. When I got home I told Mom what happened. She didn't get upset or call the police. Evil had almost seized me. We ate chicken chow mein for dinner that night and it tasted so good.

At the end of the fourth grade, Sister Mary Kenneth wrote a letter to my parents requesting that they not re-enroll me at Christ the King. They complied, and thereafter, we became "Holi-day Catholics." So, for all intents and purposes, they kicked me out of Catholic school. Most kids get kicked out of public school and transfer to Catholic school. For me, the opposite occurred. My parents grew weary from my oppositional and defiant behavior. That summer they sent me to Miami to stay with my grandparents. I lasted a week with Pop and Tita before they handed me over to my Uncle Tom; I had trespassed in the backyard of an empty house with a couple of other boys and came home soaked from head to toe, having fallen in a pond. I stayed with my uncle, Aunt Joan, and my older cousins Tommy and KC, both in high school. I'm sure my cousin Tommy tried to drown me in the pool when he dragged me into the deep end. And KC wasn't thrilled that I had to sleep in her bedroom. After a week, I flew back to New York with my uncle. He worked as a special agent with the IRS Criminal Investigation Division. I guess back then law enforcement officers could carry their firearms with them on a plane. His revolver fascinated me. As he slept, I wondered what would happen if I took it from his holster and started waving it around . . .

"This is the verdict: Light has come into the world, but people loved darkness instead of light because their deeds were evil."

JOHN 3:19

8

HOOLIGANS

LATER THAT SUMMER, I STARTED THINKING ABOUT GOING ON MY own, maybe hitchhiking to Woodstock, but I didn't want to travel alone and couldn't find anyone to accompany me. I stuck around until school began. Starting fresh at Long Acres, I thought I'd give it a chance. It first proved no different than Christ the King, and seeing no future for me in Commack, I decided to leave home. When I told Mom I planned to leave, trying to evoke some sympathy, she surprised me by offering to help pack my bag. She gave me some essentials—a couple of peanut butter and jelly sandwiches and my baseball glove—and wished me the best upon my departure. I made it as far as the cornfield, where I contemplated my plan. When the sun went down and it started getting cold, I decided to delay my trip. I thought I'd enter the house quietly through the back door but found it locked. I knocked; Mom opened the door and greeted me cheerfully, "Raymond, what's wrong? Did you forget something?" I told her I forgot to do my homework. She let me in and served me a hot dinner. I slept well that night. My only regret is not going to Woodstock.

In the fifth grade, I finally found acceptance within a group of guys at Long Acres, but I had to fight for it. No problem. I fought my whole life, but this time it got me somewhere. It started off as usual. I came to know them as Pat D., Larry, Paul, Nicky N., Richie, and Donald. Every day after school, these cigarette-smokin' delinquents jumped me on the basketball court. I'd sometimes get my shots in, break away and run like the wind down the block to get home. But if I went down, they pummeled me and left me on the ground, then walked away laughing. I came up with a new strategy: be the first to attack, get in the first punch, no big song and dance like so many big talkers, just a silent strike. So one day after class, I just walked up to the group and punched one of the leaders of the pack, Paul, in the face. He went down and none of his buddies jumped in. I caught them by surprise. After Paul conceded my victory, we dusted ourselves off and I smoked my first cigarette. The guys later turned me on to weed, and I educated them on the use of alcohol. From then on, that was my fighting style.

Tough guys, we fought each other all the time as a type of training to become tougher. And we developed other unique toughness training methods, like taking a running start and punching each other in the gut, and playing "asses-up," a variation of handball that we created. You played with as many guys who showed up, each going in turn until someone missed a return. That player then faced the wall, bent over, and each player threw the ball at the loser's butt until missing. Depending on the number or players, a guy could be up against the wall for a half-hour, depleting everyone's energy and thereby ending the game. We also verbally abused each other, an expression of macho affection.

Extremely skinny, one of the first nicknames I was given was "Bird Legs." I didn't like it and endeavored to do something about it. I discovered a set of Dad's York barbells in the basement. They must have been pressed in York, Pennsylvania, in the 1930s. Lifting became an essential part of my life—an addiction, fundamental, like breathing and eating. God used it to save me, give me strength and keep me relatively sane. Much later in life, I found the basic instruction in his Word: "Therefore, strengthen your feeble arms and your weak knees. Make level paths for your feet so that the lame may not be disabled, but rather healed." Heb 12:12. I gained strength and started putting on muscle. People noticed.

The physical part came easy, but the level paths thing took a while. I often strayed off the path going through what Dad called "The School of Hard Knocks," a refrain for my early life.

Cool guys needed girlfriends, so we started working that out. My first kiss was with Joanne in the cornfield behind the school. She was Asian and I loved her dark, almond eyes. We went into the field while everyone else hung out on the basketball court. I kissed her on the cheek and felt the electricity. The cornfield also called to the gang's reckless spirit, and we made a practice of setting it on fire, then acting like heroes trying to put it out with our hockey sticks while we waited for the fire department to arrive. It was the perfect hideout for every occasion, like toward the end of sixth grade in Mr. C's class, when Pat, Richie, Donald, and I decided to end the day early by jumping out the window and fleeing into the field. Unfortunately, I lost one of my brand-new moccasins during our great escape. When I got home, Mom used the other one to beat my ass, much to the restrained mirth of my coconspirators as they watched.

I think I began my shoplifting career in the sixth grade as well. My speed and agility made me a natural. I started off stealing bags of candy but eventually started taking orders from my friends for record albums. This winter operation required a big coat. I'd slip as many as six vinyl LPs in my coat—artists like Hendrix, The Doors, The Beatles, Iron Butterfly, and Vanilla Fudge—and quietly walk out of Modell's Shopper's World. I liked stealing, the thrill of it. Modell's hired some young security guards, guys in their late teens and early twenties. One day I walked out of the store with a bag of candy peanuts, and one of the guards followed me out. He tried sneaking up on me a few feet from the door, but I took off, dropping the candy to free my arms as I burst into full sprinting mode. He chased me around the back of the store and through the opening in the fence near the sump that led into the neighborhood. I burned him badly by the time I entered the cornfield. As I caught my breath between stalks along the side path, I saw that he commandeered David and his bike with the banana seat and chopper handlebars. He hadn't taken full control; he gassed, and David gave him a ride on the handlebars. I caught up with David a few days later, and my fists let him know how I felt about his assistance.

"People do not despise a thief if he steals to satisfy his hunger when he is starving."

PROVERBS 6:30

9

BULLIES AND BATTLES

I STARTED SEVENTH GRADE AT JFK JUNIOR HIGH SCHOOL, ON THE other end of town. Junior high offered class periods, locker rooms, and mandatory showers after gym. This is where bullying became intensified because a kid could be cornered, even stuffed in a locker with no place to run. Wedgies and wet towel whippings occurred routinely. Two asshole eighth graders terrorized me the entire school year. Older kids evoked a new kind of fear, and I experienced a freeze state, rather than the fight or flight I knew. I kept lifting in the basement and tried out for the football team, since my speed made me a sandlot star on the block. However, I never played tackle football with equipment before and realized a new level of contact. I weighed about 115 pounds and tried out for cornerback. On my very first play during a scrimmage, the tight end, an eighth grader who outweighed me by 50 pounds, charged off the line and knocked me on my ass. This reaffirmed a lesson I already learned—hit or be hit.

My battles with John D. also began in the seventh grade. John was a fringe member of the gang from Long Acres, and we shared an intense dislike for each other. By seventh grade, he already stood six-feet tall and weighed 200 pounds. During that first fight, he retaught me the element of surprise. Remember, hit or be hit, because if you got hit hard enough on the first hit, you'd keep getting hit and never get in a hit. We stood in the front lobby at JFK waiting for the afternoon buses when he ambushed me in the foyer to the auditorium. Caught in a tight space, I was leaning back against the wall when he knocked the books out of my hands. Before I could react, he grabbed me and slammed me against the wall, which stunned me as I dropped to the floor. Each time I tried to get up, he'd grab me again and throw me against the wall until I went out on my feet, essentially unable to defend myself. He destroyed me.

We ran into each other that weekend on the playground at Long Acres, where we hung out and smoked cigarettes. When he showed up, Pat, who could often inspire me to fight, got in my ear and convinced me that if I didn't fight John right then and there I'd be seen as a pussy for the rest of my life. So I called him out. Only this time I seized the advantages: the open space and the blazing speed of my footwork and fists. I knew I could take him as long as I stayed away from his meaty hands. I boxed his ears off, dancing around, throwing left jabs and straight rights to his face. When he bull rushed me, I just stepped aside and hit him again. I didn't have any real power, but I had plenty of energy. John was fat, and after a minute or so of being punched in the face and running around trying to tackle me, he was totally gassed and sat his fat ass down on the merry-go-round, breathing heavily. I thought the fight was over as everyone could see, but Pat got in my ear and taught me how to fight dirty. He urgently whispered, "Hit him! Hit him right now!" "But Pat, he's done. He can't even stand up." "Hit him! Fuck up his face so he'll know not to ever fuck with you again." Pat convinced me. I took a running start and punched John in his right eye, blowing it up and sending him home crying. He moped around school for the next two weeks with a black eye. Ironically, I would have my last fight with John when I was nineteen.

The girls developed more quickly than the boys in seventh grade, which expanded my masturbatory fantasy life. I sat next to Sherry in biology class. One of the cool kids, she was already a beautiful, full-bodied woman. One day when the bell rang, signaling the changing of classes, I stayed in my seat until my erection subsided and told my teacher I wasn't feeling well and just needed a couple of minutes.

In eighth grade, all the kids from my side of town attended the newly constructed Burr Junior High, named after Aaron Burr, who shot and killed Alexander Hamilton in a dual. Burr Mansion was down Burr Road, and I thought Aaron Burr was cool. They took down the cornfield behind Long Acres to build the school, making it walking distance from my house and providing me an opportunity to expand my drinking. My parents stocked a full liquor cabinet, and I learned that if I drank shots from each of the different bottles, they wouldn't notice any missing alcohol. I drank vodka, Scotch whiskey, bourbon, tequila, and gin. I started pouring liquor into a small Tupperware container (also used for salad dressing) and taking sips while walking to school. Sometimes I invited a friend to meet me at the swings at Long Acres to drink before going to class. I didn't do it every day and handled it pretty well until the day I drank a little too much and passed out at my desk, drooling. My teacher sent me to the dean's office. Mr. K. didn't know I had been drinking (I guess the mints did the job) but asked if I knew about LSD. The school contacted my parents, but I don't remember them being too concerned.

I put on a lot of muscle over the summer and earned a starting cornerback position on the football team. No longer being bullied, I tried bullying to see what it felt like. A couple of times I cornered pudgy Mark P. in the boy's room and faked like I was going to punch him in the face. I never hit him; I could see that he was scared, and I felt stupid.

There were five distinct groups in junior and senior high: the stoners or heads (evolved from the hippies), featuring long hair, bellbottom blue jeans, and flannel or paisley shirts; the greasers, who wore white tee shirts (with a pack of cigarettes folded in the sleeve), black leather jackets and heavy black boots with steel toes; the jocks, clean cut and presentable; the nerds, who wore glasses and pocket pencil holders in their plaid shirts; and the disco boys. I was primarily a disco boy in junior and senior high school, when it suited me. We rocked shag haircuts, shirts with bright patterns, polyester pants (with a slight bell), a short brown leather jacket and platform heels . . . the higher the better. Looking back, it is clear that the disco boys featured the most ridiculous style.

"For everything in the world—the lust of the flesh, the lust of the eyes, and the pride of life—comes not from the Father but the world."

1 JOHN 2:16

10

EARLY CRIMINAL HISTORY

MY FIRST ARREST HAPPENED AT THE AGE OF THIRTEEN. I GOT A job that summer as a dishwasher at Bishop McDonald's Camp, located on the other side of the then cornfield, a Fresh Air Fund program run by the Franciscan Brothers from some parish in Brooklyn. Kids from Brooklyn and the Bronx would stay there for two weeks every summer. I sported a mustache by then and listed my age on the application as sixteen. I earned some spending cash and bought a dime bag of weed. Having my own stash made me excited to get high with my friends. That Saturday afternoon, I bought some rolling papers and decided to sit in the alcove to the back door of Long Acres and roll the whole bag up into joints. So I sat there and rolled away, oblivious to the presence of the maintenance man, mopping the school hallway and standing a few feet away watching me from the other side of the glass doors. I planned to be an expert at rolling by the time I completed the task. He called the cops, and before I finished the job, a squad car came racing around the back of the school and blocked me in. This time I didn't have a chance to run. The cop placed me in handcuffs behind my back and put me in the front seat. As we drove to the Fourth Precinct, he told me how I was going to be a hard kid after I got out of reform school. The scared-straight act continued at the precinct. They put me in a room with a two-way mirror and handcuffed me to a chair. This didn't impress me, and I kept flipping off whoever was behind the mirror. I acted like a tough guy. Mom came and picked me up.

Mom first demonstrated her psychic abilities the summer before my sophomore year at Commack North. My buddies and I were getting ready to make the two-mile bike ride to the high school for JV football practice. We all rode ten-speed racing bikes and carried our equipment bags. A single rope looped from the bottom of my bag to the top, so I hung it around one shoulder. Mom told me to be careful that it didn't slip off and get caught in the spokes of the front wheel. I said "Sure, Mom," and we took off. Burr Road, a single-lane road, took us all downhill. We were flying, and as always, I led the pack. About halfway down, just as Mom warned, my bag slipped off my shoulder, got caught in the spokes of the front wheel, and launched me head over heels into the middle of the street. While all this happened, a family drove by in a station wagon alongside us. As my body did a full flip in the air, I caught a glimpse of the man driving the car as he turned the steering wheel to his left as hard as he could. His eyes were wide open. And just as I landed on my back, I could see the treads of the right front tire as it narrowly missed my face. I rolled to my feet and stepped to the side of the road. I survived, relatively unscathed, but the man said he almost had a heart attack after checking to see if there were any injuries. We made it to school on time for practice, and I busted my butt during drills. I could barely walk the next day. This was the first of a number of near-death moments.

A much more powerful demonstration of Mom's maternal psychic senses involved my sister during the fall of her senior year in 1975. Two weeks after school began, Teresa went out for a night of partying with her boyfriend, Billy, and our friend Mark H. Mark drove his van, and Teresa and Billy sat in the open back of the vehicle on a carpeted bench. They were hit head on by a drunk driver. Mom worked that night in the ER, doing her normal graveyard shift. The ER nurses were a tight group. They saw the carnage carried in each shift—motor vehicle accidents, gunshot and sharp-edged weapon wounds, torn and broken bodies, some dead on arrival. Many of the patients they treated were high school students, and many of the nurses had children the same age. They supported each other with love and humor, trusting their own kids would be safe. Around the specific time of the accident, Mom knew that something happened to Teresa, something bad. Her coworkers tried to calm her down and talk reasonably about how they all shared the same worries but that it would be ok. Mom insisted and persisted that she knew something was very wrong, something terrible. She felt some part of the trauma Teresa experienced as the impact of the collision tossed her around the open back of the van like a rag doll, ripping the flesh from her forehead. Fifteen minutes after Mom started sharing her feelings, the ER received a call from St. John's Hospital in Smithtown reporting the accident. Her injuries weren't critical, and upon Mom's request, they transported Teresa to Huntington Hospital. Surgery reattached Teresa's forehead leaving a scar that would fade away over time, but the emotional scars took many years to heal.

I became a chameleon in high school and varied my style depending on whom I chose to be with. The constant theme, however, was to look cool and show off my muscles. I wore black-rimmed glasses and my hair down to my shoulders at one point. I got along with everybody except a few racist assholes. I played JV baseball, football, and trombone. I learned to play in the junior high band/orchestra. I chose the instrument because the large mouthpiece fit my big lips. Also, I used it not only as an instrument, but as a weapon. In marching band, I enjoyed knocking Mark P.'s hat off during rehearsals.

I also joined the Pep Band during basketball season to be near Paula. I first gazed upon her beauty in junior high school when the girl's gymnastics team from crosstown-rival JFK competed at Burr. I noticed her long blond hair, her beautiful face, green eyes, and her athletic body, highlighted by her tights. She performed on the uneven bars, and I commented on the shape of her buttocks to a kid from JFK, who happened to be her brother, Willy. The conversation ended quickly. I later learned that Paula was the oldest of six kids; she was twelve years older than her youngest sibling and only sister, Carla. She also came from an alcoholic home. Her parents met as students at Columbia, where her mother, Gloria, was the only woman in the chemistry department; her father, Bill, was a psychology major. Her mother never finished college, and her father went into banking after graduating and found himself done in by the two-hour martini business lunches. He occasionally would not come home after work. His drinking made it challenging for him to keep a job and even though Paula's family lived in a large five-bedroom house in one of the nicer parts of town, bills went unpaid and they ate a lot of spaghetti. Gloria left with the children twice. The first time, they moved into an apartment in Parkway Village, Queens. The separation lasted a couple of years when Paula was in first and second grade.

Inspired by her compassion and counseling instincts, Paula was naturally drawn to lovable bad boys with a heart. Her high school boyfriend ended up receiving a life sentence for killing a jewelry store owner during an attempted robbery while he was out on parole. Her story with *this* bad boy, by the grace of God, is happier.

Nixon's resignation on August 9, 1974, following Watergate, both affirmed and inspired my rebellious spirit. I was almost fifteen and nobody could tell me anything. The president was a crook, and you couldn't trust "The Man." By the time I entered eleventh grade, the Hooligans expanded to include about thirty-five guys. We officially claimed the name from a local newspaper article about a home invasion. Some crazy kid stole some weed from a hooligan's stash. The hooligan and friends found him at his house, forced their way in, ripped the phone off the wall, and destroyed a bunch of furniture. The article headline read: "Hooligans Terrorize Commack Resident."

Starting on Friday nights, we spent weekends partying, getting drunk and high, and looking for unsupervised house parties to crash. At one such party, I experienced my first encounter with a switchblade. Drunk off my ass, I stumbled out of the house onto the driveway with some of the varsity football players. I saw a couple of greasers, Joe and Chris, standing on the driveway in front of Joe's blue Charger, one of the fastest muscle cars in town. Joe, also a Hooligan, was shitfaced drunk and pissed off. I went over to ask about the problem, and they started yelling about somebody throwing rocks at Joe's car. I tried to talk to Joe, but he didn't recognize me. Then Chris pressed what I thought was his finger on my chest, yelling at me and accusing me of throwing rocks. I prepared to fight him. Even in a drunken stupor, I possessed good fighting instincts; I kept quiet and always tried to hit first, but as my teammates pulled me away, I saw that it wasn't his finger in my chest but Chris brandished a switchblade, now waving it back and forth in front of my face. My buddies pulled me into a car, and we drove away. When I sobered up I felt grateful, not revengeful. I had never encountered a knife before and held no interest in confronting my assailant, whose memory of the event seemed unlikely. I was crazy but not stupid.

Football served as a great outlet for my anger. I started at outside linebacker my junior year. We placed third in the pre-season Suffolk County ranking but ended up having a .500 record. We lacked leadership, starting with the head coach, Mr. D. He stood 5'2"—a solid tree trunk of a man—and earned All-State linebacker accolades at Central Islip (CI) in his prime. A one-man wrecking crew fueled by his very low center of gravity, he used his crazy, angry, little man complex to inspire his players with violence, pounding his fists into the sides of our helmets and throwing cans of "Stickem" at us. My best game came on a Friday night at Central Islip, a tough minority community, 90-percent Black and Hispanic. I scored my only touchdown that night. Their fullback fumbled at midfield; the ball bounced right into my hands, on the run, and I ran a clear path to the end zone after stiff-arming the quarterback. As I raced the fifty yards, I heard the crowd roar in response and ran faster. It was very cool. The home field refs blew the call and gave us possession . . . but not the score. The coaches gave me the assignment to cover their All-State wide receiver, Lem McCray, who eventually accepted a Division-I scholarship to play lacrosse at Syracuse. We played a different, more violent game in the 70s. You could use your helmet to spear your opponent and clothesline or horse collar a player. On his only reception of the game, I horse collared Lem on a screen pass that only gained five yards. We lost by a touchdown, but the real action came after the game. They started shooting out the windows of our bus as we pulled away. Everybody ducked for cover. Only when the driver stopped at a red light at the corner did we realize that we left Nicky T. behind. He came running up, still wearing his helmet, and when he jumped into the bus, we broke out into that raucous, nervous laughter of release.

Mr. S.—my favorite teacher, the real deal, an ex-Marine drill sergeant—could beat the shit out of anybody in the school, or on the street for that matter and 250 pounds of solid Marine muscle, I'm guessing he was in his mid-to-late 40s. A loving, Christian man, he cared about his students. He came from somewhere down south and spoke with a slow drawl. He taught trigonometry. He liked me and believed in my potential, which is why he selected me to be a member of his President's Physical Fitness Team. I trained for a little while but blew it off and let him down. As far as math goes, Mr. S. proved to be the second-smartest person I knew. Dad only took a few minutes to solve one of our take-home assignments, the "Unsolvable Problem." Dad, also a great teacher, could take the most complicated equation and break it down into the simplest terms that almost anyone could learn and explain. I proudly put it up on the blackboard, copying the equation Dad had written out, and even though I explained how I arrived at the solution, Mr. S. knew my dad had solved the problem. But he didn't confront me in front of the class. That wasn't his way.

Mr. S. could be quite forceful. If you arrived late for class, he made you stand against the back wall. As he strolled around toward the back of the room, speaking out the lesson, he'd suddenly turn and punch the wall—inches from your face—the sound reverberating in your eardrum, and ask, "Why were you late, boy?" But before you could give an answer, he'd bark out an order to drop and give him twenty, during which he'd press his foot into the middle of your back for added resistance.

Kevin, a greaser in my trig class, kept giving me shit about my ancestry. I wasn't the only crazy in school, and he kept coming at me to make a name for himself with his boys. One day, he dogged me in front of his friends under the safety of the bell alerting us to report for seventh period. Undone, I followed him into class, and as he sat down, I began reigning hammer fists on top of his head. Mr. S. stood on the other side of the room, greeting his students at the door, like he always did. He immediately charged through the middle of the room, tossing desks aside like Moses parting the Red Sea. He swiftly placed me in an arm bar and walked me down to the dean's office. Mr. S. was the head dean. He didn't suspend me, but lectured me on the lethal nature of the hammer fist, which could be deadly if landed against the base of the neck at the top of the trapezoid muscle with enough force to crush the carotid artery. I never forgot that lesson.

"Slash to the right, you sword, then to the left, wherever
your blade is turned."

EZEKIEL 21:16

11

THE GREAT SINK INCIDENT

IN SPITE OF MY MANY DISTRACTIONS, I WANTED TO PLEASE MR. S. by acing the midterm. In preparation for the test, I stopped partying for a couple of weeks and actually studied my trig problems. I took a break one night and went to see *One Flew Over the Cuckoo's Nest,* starring Jack Nicholson as R.P. McMurphy and Louise Fletcher as Nurse Ratched. For the first time in my life, I felt inspired by a film, and Jack Nicholson became my favorite actor. On the day of the test, I came in with confidence, but my mind went completely blank when I stared at the problems on paper. Perhaps I put too much pressure on myself or was just a pathetic burnout. Regardless, as the bell sounded, I walked out enraged. Mr. S.'s classroom was on the second floor, and after the bell sounded, I walked down the hall toward the front of the school, kicking and punching lockers on the way. I entered the boys' restroom near the stairwell and grabbed the middle sink, both hands locked on like a vice. I was alone. I noticed my rapid breathing, the tension throughout my body, and the screaming in my brain. "Shitttt!" Then a vision came; I pictured the Chief at the end of the movie. I watched in my mind as he wrapped his arms around the huge water cooler. My heart began beating faster as he ripped the cooler from its foundation, lifted it to his shoulder and hurled it through the caged window.

And as the Chief escaped and slowly jogged off into the woods on his way to Canada—to freedom—I knew what I needed to do. I began to pull at the sides of the sink, mustering all the strength I possessed. I heard the pipes begin to break and the sound of spraying water; my strength surged. I ripped the sink free and carried it to the window, left open wide enough for me to toss it out into the courtyard below. I was apparently oblivious to the school layout at the time, and didn't know whether anyone had been placed in any danger by my inspired purge. Water gushed from the broken pipe and rushed across the floor into the hallway.

If I turned left to exit the bathroom, I could've easily run down the stairs and out the front door, undetected. Instead, I turned right and ran down the hall, past all the classrooms and all the teachers who emerged after hearing the commotion. I ran down the back stairwell, catching my breath, and casually walked into the cafeteria. Eighth period was free for both Mr. S. and me, and he usually lounged in the Dean's Office. I'm sure he received a quick report on my crime because as I walked out of the cafeteria, munching on an ice cream sandwich, he came heading straight toward me. We stopped; he looked me straight in the eyes—like he always did—and asked, "You been doing something wrong, boy?" to which I found my head nodding in affirmation. They suspended me for three days, and I paid for *two* sinks because the sink I tore from the wall smashed the one to the right of it.

The Great Sink Incident cemented my legacy. Some thought if I could rip a sink from the wall, I could break a guy's neck. I eventually became aware of the Great Sink Incident as experienced by others. Mrs. Calabro taught Spanish in a classroom directly below the boys' room, and she liked to look out across the courtyard when teaching her class. Eyewitnesses reported that when the sink came crashing down a few feet from where she stood, she jumped, shrieked like a woman in a horror movie, and took quite some time to calm herself down. She dismissed her class early. On the opposite side of the courtyard, a couple of stoners—think Cheech and Chong, staring out the second floor window of their biology class, high as kites—saw the sink fall from the window to the courtyard, turned to each other and had the following exchange: "Dude, did you just see that sink fly out the window?" "Yeah man, that was so cool!"

For some reason, by the start of my senior year, they still hadn't replaced the sinks. One day, I walked into the same bathroom to find a group of sophomores gathered. Four or five of the little dudes stood facing me, listening to their buddy giving an "eyewitness" account. He described the event in detail, the sound and the rushing water. Then he noticed that his friends' attention focused on something behind him. I realized the kid's instincts functioned well when he rhetorically asked, "He's standing right behind me, isn't he?" They simultaneously nodded in affirmation and slowly, silently walked past me and exited the bathroom like little ducks in a row. After The Great Sink Incident, my guidance counselor worked out a therapeutic program which allowed me to leave school any time I felt angry or anxious. And ten years later, when Paula and I were living in Southern California, she received a call from her younger brother, Michael, a student at Commack North. He asked if the sink incident really happened and became concerned about his sister's safety upon hearing the truth.

The Great Sink Incident brought me a lot of attention. People looked at me expressing a new level of fear and curiosity. Teachers averted eye contact, except for Mr. S. Even Tony felt threatened. Friends and competitive rivals, I could beat Tony in a sprint, but he surpassed me in strength. He was tough and had beaten up a lot of guys. One day, we started roughhousing in the cafeteria and Tony shoved me toward the wall separating the cafeteria from the courtyard. It was lined with heavy glass windows, and kids often sat on the floor along the wall. Tony pushed me toward two girls sitting between two windows. In order to avoid crashing into them, I side-stepped them to the left, and my momentum carried my head through the window, smashing through the drone of casual conversations. Immediately afterward, someone got a plastic chair for me and I sat down, bleeding profusely from a large laceration on the top of my head. A crowd gathered around, pressing in, gawking in amazement and disgust. Being the center of their attention angered me. I saw a significant amount of blood pooled on the chair between my legs and slapped it, splattering blood upon the onlookers who recoiled and shrieked in terror. Coach D. showed up and walked by my side as they transported me to the nurse's office, nervously joking about getting me a larger helmet.

The nurse bandaged my wound, and the Commack Volunteer Ambulance Corp showed up to take me to the hospital. Mom and our next-door neighbor, Jenny, were founding members of the Corps, and Jenny happened to be the driver that day. Mom was working a swing shift at the ER. I'm pretty sure Jenny launched the ambulance fully airborne as we drove over the small, steep hill crossing the railroad tracks. The ER visit turned into an episode of *The Twilight Zone* with Rod Sterling. The nurse unwrapped my bandage and started to laugh, which confused me and caused some concern. Were my brains hanging out, causing her to have a nervous breakdown? The nightmare got worse when she gathered the other nurses on duty to take a look, and they also began to laugh. Was this some type of mass hysteria! Mom finally arrived and allayed my fears by explaining that the nurse at the school had used a tampon to dress my wound, and her coworkers just found this to be the funniest thing. I didn't think it was funny.

My mom was tough. I guess with me as a son, she had to be. One enchanted evening we were taking bong hits in my bedroom in the basement and blowing the smoke out the window. I know big Brian S. was there. We were both big-time partiers and our endurance was infamous. Depending on your body chemistry, experience and ambition, one could drink a tremendous amount of alcohol, do a ton of drugs, and remain conscious and functional in your own mind. Now that doesn't include blackouts, of which I had many I don't care to remember. Getting back to the bong party in my room, Johnny R. brought some Rum & Coke and we were mixing drinks in the bathroom. Why we weren't doing that in my bedroom I don't know. Just stupid. Before going to work for her graveyard shift, Mom came down to remind me that my friends and I had to leave. She stopped in the bathroom first and discovered our toilet & sink bar. Of course I was playing records on my turntable, probably *Wish You Were Here,* Pink Floyd's new album, so we couldn't hear but the last three knocks on the wooden door that caused the record to skip. I opened the door and went out to talk to Mom. I don't remember what she said. But I do remember part of what she said to my friends. After I reentered the room, everyone quietly asked, almost whispered, "What did she say? What did she say?" Mom burst into the room and answered "I'll tell you what she said, right from *The Horse's Mouth!*" I don't remember what she said after that and neither did my friends. However, they could never forget the evil eye cast upon them. I was used to it but it left a lasting impression on the stoners.

We also played pool in the basement, where I honed my skills in 8-Ball. One Saturday afternoon, we were playing for money. A primary rule of my residency as the beast in the basement: I couldn't leave my shit upstairs, especially my shoes. As I lined up the winning shot, the basement door opened, and Mom threw my boots down the stairs. They hit the end of the cue stick, causing me to scratch on the shot and lose the game. My friends started laughing and I got pissed off, picked up the boots and launched them up the stairs, smashing against the door. The door opened and Mom slowly descended the steps. I leaned back against the end of the pool table, the cue stick in my hands, trying to be cool in front of my buddies. She swiftly grabbed the stick and smacked me over the head several times, rendering me stunned and seeing stars; she then placed the stick back in my hands, which helped me maintain my balance as she ascended the stairs. My friends followed her up silently and exited through the back door. Thereafter, any time I invited people to come over to party or shoot pool, they always asked, "Is your mom going to be home?"

"Then Samson reached toward the two central pillars on which the temple stood. Bracing himself against them, his right hand on the one and his left hand on the other . . . he pushed with all his might, and down came the temple . . ."

JUDGES 16:29, 30

12

SATURDAY NIGHT'S ALRIGHT
FOR FIGHTING

THE HOOLIGANS OFFERED POWER, ALWAYS READY TO FIGHT WITH
Commack South or Kings Park, the next town over. And we knew
where to find trouble—the Commack Drive Inn, where everyone
hung out. One Friday night, we got into it against some guys from
South. The irrelevance of who started it and why notwithstand-
ing, it often involved a guy from North seeing someone's girlfriend
from South and vice versa. We outnumbered them at least two to
one and beat them down, all fists and feet, but rough stuff; heads
kicked in, broken ribs, and so it goes. Later that night, we reveled
at Silo Park, near the high school. We flew high as kites, drinking,
smoking weed, and pumping each other up, when one of our guys
drove into the parking lot and reported seeing Southsiders waiting for us in front of Carmela's, with bats, bottles, and who knows
what. Carmela's . . . *our* hangout! I jumped in the front passenger
seat of Joe's Charger, the fastest car in our group. I found a crowbar
on the floor and grabbed it, feeling the cold iron in my hand.

"The Rumble"

The blue Charger roars
into the parking lot.
Tires squealing
in the pain of burning rubber.
headlights glaring
grill gleaming like silver fangs
tears into the pack of stunned warriors,
who scatter like a flock of scared crows.
The slower ones thud off the hood.

The rest of North
spreads into South
like a school of blood-frenzied sharks.
The bronze warrior at the front swings a crowbar
like a windmill in the fury of a storm.
An enemy comes up from behind
and smashes the bronzeman
crowning his head with a bottle.
He is blinded, for a moment,
by a shower of screaming glass.

When his eyes clear
from the blood that he tastes
he sees his homeboys
swarming upon the fallen few
like mad hornets stinging bloodied meat,
their boots banging out
a beat of muffled grunts.
Enraged,
he pushes them aside
and hammers away
at some long, scraggly black hair,
matted against a bloody head.
The skull cracks.
His crowbar splashes deeper
splattering blood in the night.

A siren's wail disperses the angry swarm.
The crimson crowbar slips from his bloody hand;
he is pulled away.
The gang scurries to their cars

and retreats to the woods
where they guzzle down brew around a fire.
They brag about their feats,
exaggerating each blow,
and search each other's eyes for acceptance.

The bronze warrior sits in a shroud of ice
and searches the fire for his soul.

Then, I envisioned myself a romantic warrior; not a drunken fool. We never left the parking lot. My head wound caused a lot of bleeding. I stood with some friends who tried to examine the extent of my injury, when a guy approached to see if he could help. I punched him a few times and knocked him to the ground. He got up and ran away. The cops arrived in full force by this time and I, in full-blown crazed idiot mode, couldn't keep my mouth shut. They handcuffed me and placed me in the back seat of a patrol car, where I proceeded to try to kick out the side window. Out of my mind, I ended up the only one from North taken to the ER, but a bunch of guys from South received treatment for their injuries, some with broken bones and fractured skulls. We saw each other. I caught a few stitches, and I'm assuming Mom picked me up. I don't remember, but I remember the next night.

A planned event, one of our guys had contacted one of their guys and set up the rumble to happen at one of their hangouts, the parking lot of a small strip mall on Commack Road. It was a Saturday night, and we had six carloads of guys. I brought the bottom half of an aluminum cue stick that I grabbed from the basement. I thought it would make a good weapon. Let's just say that Elton John was on the radio singing *Saturday Night's Alright for Fighting*. When we pulled into the lot, there were a dozen or so guys from South at the far end near a dirt hill that led into some woods. We jumped out of our cars and bolted across the lot, screaming like wild banshees. Their guys ran up the hill and into the woods; we chased them to the top clearing, which was fully lit by streetlights. Not stupid enough to follow them into unfamiliar woods, we started screaming out obscenities instead, calling them "fucking pussies." Our drunken, stoned frenzy rendered us oblivious to the cars that had pulled into the lot and the firing line that had emerged from the vehicles. They set us up. I was the first to notice puffs of dirt exploding around our feet with a ricochet, the first to notice the firing squad that had formed with a half-dozen guys with rifles, and the first to act.

I made a command decision and led a brilliant counterattack of throwing rocks in response. I also quickly realized the absolute idiocy of that action. It's fortunate they couldn't shoot well and a miracle no one got hit. I ordered the second course of action and led our charge down the hill onto Commack Road, to come around and flank our enemies. We came together, thirty strong, and faced off against South, forty and stronger. No flanking to be done; there was a line between the two groups, like in *West Side Story*, but with more guys. As always, I stood right up front, but this time something different took place—I became captivated by the guy straight across from me. I didn't recognize him. He looked older, maybe in his early 20s, and he held a massive chain, about six feet long with thick links, swinging it around above his head, around and around, the full length of the chain just a few feet away. I became spellbound by the swinging of that chain, around and around, and the bottom end of a cue stick no longer seemed like such a good weapon. I was afraid, with my mind spinning around and around as that chain swung around and around. The sound of sirens broke the spell; everyone ran as the cops pulled up in full force. Fast in flight, I didn't get arrested . . . that night.

During this time of reckless rage, Mom remained relentless in her challenge to reel me in. She knew the value of documenting a "permanent record," which I'm sure was somewhat therapeutic for her. From January 1 through December 28, 1976, she kept a journal of the actions of me and my sister, which documented her efforts to confront, reprimand, and institute punitive consequences. I didn't respond well as concisely reported in this entry from April 21: "*Spoke to Ray about late hours— doesn't think they are so late and Called me Dearie (very sarcastically)." Her description of the drive-in fight and subsequent rumble offer a different perspective. On May 14, she wrote, "Ray went to movies w Ed H @

drive in / Got into a fight at drive in / 'Had to help a friend' / left & got into another fight at shopping center armed w a tire iron. Got arrested $25 bail." This is clearly a more concise, well-written account of that Friday night, and the pride she expressed in her May 21 entry showed the hope she held for my future: "Ray made the papers today—story of arrest—page 1 of Commack News! Wanted his money 'His damn money!' Spent $11 yesterday (owed Larry $10) request denied / left @ 7 00 for Larry's house & to hang out @ park / Came home @ 1 10 A / Was riding around w friends and drinking." Mom's journal reveals her "tough love," strength, humor, and endurance.

Mom also remained relentless in investigating my bad conduct. She excelled, and her search and seizure missions through my bedroom bagged a lot of the weed I hid in ceiling panels and clothing pockets. Uncle George, a well-known pothead, benefited from her work. Rather than flush my shit, she gave it to her brother for "testing" purposes. Years later, he commented on the high quality of my stash. Mom's policing method used silence as a psychological weapon. She never confronted me with her findings and knew that any accusations on my part would be an admission of guilt. So we played this game, and I developed some counter methods for deterrence that demonstrated worthiness. Survival, or "Snorkel" jackets, were very popular in the '70s. Usually army green with a fur-lined hood, the coat featured approximately forty individual pockets. It served as a useful place to hide joints, pipes, rolling papers, etc., and had been an obvious target of Mom's successful raids. So, I cut up forty small pieces of paper, wrote "fuck you" on each one and placed them in all the pockets. Mom found them—everyone one of them. When she later told family and friends the story, she always ended with, "And I'll be damned if he didn't put a 'fuck you' in every single pocket." I believe she actually felt some pride in my thoroughness and defiant passion.

Dad spoke prophetically into my life during all of this: "You're going through the school of hard knocks. I see three things happening to you; either you're going to jail, the nut house, or you're going to end up dead." His prophecy rang true as all three came to be, but he never got in my face about it. He never confronted me forcefully. But he was a persistent philosopher and consistently spoke his teachings into all of us. His holy trinity was mind, body, and personality, which over his lifetime evolved and transformed into mind, body, and love. He was also a believer in the Golden Mean and would preach, "When you're down, don't get too down because you're always going to have your ups. And when you're up, don't get too up because you're always going to have your downs." And Dad was a problem solver. Professionally, he was known as the guy to go to when you're stumped, when you tried everything you know and everything you've learned during the problem-solving process and you're done. Then it was time to go to Fred, who was always working on his own projects but was always ready to help. And he would go at it from every possible angle, always thinking *out of the box*. He was doggedly tenacious, relentlessly smart, and he would solve the problem. If there was a problem he couldn't solve, I never heard of it. That's why he has over fifty patents and every award in the industry; that's why they named an antenna after him; that's why engineering students read about *The Lopez Feed* in their textbooks. This was how Dad approached all aspects of his life.

Dad exploded on rare occasions, like the day I stood on the back steps and cursed out my brother, Steve, for some long-forgotten offense. Maybe he failed to pull his quota of weeds. I was dropping the F-bomb when Dad came around the side of the house. He didn't see Steve and charged at me, thinking I was cursing out Mom. He started pounding away, throwing lefts and rights to my head. I tried to block the blows, and Mom came to the back door and yelled, "Freddie! What are you doing?" Dad stopped as if awakening from a dream and tried to hug me, saying he was sorry. I pushed him away and headed out. Mom never gave up on me. The only person who could look me straight in the eyes at that point in my life, she never showed fear. Everyone else was afraid; *I* was afraid. I confronted my fears head-on, by being crazy so that everyone would fear me. And it worked.

My parents tried to assert some semblance of control after the rumble and my arrest. They grounded me for a week. I complied, but for the night a hooligan came to my basement/bedroom window and told me that the Scanga twins were waiting for me down the street in the parking lot of Long Acres, saying I was a punk for using a crowbar. Back then, if anyone called you a punk, you had to fight; otherwise you'd be called a pussy for the rest of your life. I climbed out the window, jumped in my buddy's car, and we arrived at the school in seconds. The car hadn't even stopped when I jumped out and ran toward the Scangas with both fists clenched. Tall and heavyset, they each weighed about 230 pounds and had that long, scraggly black hair. One of them had a bandage over his head. Tony attempted to mediate; everyone saw me and Tony as sort of co-leaders of the Hooligans. O'Brien, a notorious tough guy, crazy criminal from South, stood by the Scangas. As I ran toward them, one of them yelled, "Punk!" Tony attempted to calm things down, saying, "Wait a minute; nobody here's a punk." I said nothing, just ran up and got into my fighting stance, bouncing a bit on my feet. I decided not to hit first because of the double threat, which gave me pause to think. My temporary sobriety also helped in the cognitive fighting process. They didn't want to fight. They didn't know me, but they saw the fire in my eyes—plus I weighed in at a jacked 175 pounds.

Much ado about nothing. I walked home and climbed in through the basement window. Dad knew something and must've gone down to the basement; he called me upstairs. He never called for me. I knew I had to tell him the truth, but I thought my story presented better if I could show some blood drawn for defending my honor. So I punched myself in the face three or four times, cutting my lip. He didn't believe me. I never fought the Scangas again, but some tense moments lay ahead. My sister went to South because of the excellent art program, and most of her friends came from there. One night, she threw a birthday party in the back yard. The Scangas and some other toughs from South crashed. We saw each other but nothing happened, and I left before I did something to ruin the party.

And so it goes; going to school, playing football, drinking, drugging, fighting, and working. Amphetamines came into my life—Black Beauties, White 697s; I loved to speed and drink and smoke weed. I washed dishes at my first real job, then worked as a busboy at Mt. Fuji's Japanese Steakhouse in Huntington. I worked hard, and all that soap and hot water got rid of my warts, which let me feel a little less guilt about masturbating. The cops ate for free at Mt. Fuji's, a crazy place where all the chefs were illegals from Japan. I loved celebrating a customer's birthday by shouting Bonsai, surrounding the table, and singing "Happy Birthday" in a fake Japanese accent, alongside the singing chefs. One time, two of the chefs got into a full-on Kung Fu fight over a waitress, straight out of a Bruce Lee movie. I watched excitedly as they threw side kicks and punches, avoiding each other's strikes and punching holes in the walls, before I stepped between them and broke it up. The manager appreciated it. Me and my coworkers, who were also a couple of my stoner friends, took full advantage of the opportunities offered by this shady establishment, like stealing a case of Kiren Beer every Friday and Saturday night. On one occasion, we found the basement door locked and accidently broke a window trying to force it open. The manager came down and found us; we quickly explained that we finished stocking the beer when we accidentally broke the window. He kept repeating, "Something funny, something funny." And he was right—there was always something funny going on at Mt. Fuji's.

"Honor your father and mother"—which is the first commandment with a promise—"so that it may go well with you and that you may enjoy long life on the earth."

EPHESIANS 6: 2,3

13

THE SECOND KNIFE INCIDENT

THE SECOND TIME I FACED A KNIFE-BRANDISHING PUNK OC-
curred at Salt's Pub in Northport. Frequented by people from
Commack, Elwood, and Northport, Salt's offered another spot
where trouble could be found. It featured a narrow floor space,
containing a pool table, foosball table, and three or four tables for
seating on a raised level, lined by a decorative metal railing. I arrived that night accompanied by the usual suspects, including my
best friend, Eddie. Capable of doing anything when together, at
times we egged each other on to engage in some form of frenzied
destruction. We dropped some acid that night and having a mellow trip, seeing trails, everything was groovy. We felt nothing but
the love that night, until it changed, like the Alice Cooper song,
"Welcome to My Nightmare." "*I think you're going to like it.*"

We sat down at a table where a couple of empty beer mugs
had been left behind. Then a group of guys confronted us. Their
leader, a muscular wrestler type, wearing a full black beard, stood
over me and told us to get the fuck out of their seats. Still floating
in the mellow yellow acid glow, I asked if he and his friends could
kindly sit at one of the empty tables nearby. In a flash, he pulled
out one of those butterfly blades and started whipping it around
like Bruce Lee. It made a rhythmic clinging sound as the blade

swung back and forth between the golden handles. He must have practiced a lot. His demonstration continued, and we thought it best to relinquish our seats, after which he snapped his blade shut, placed it in his pocket and sat down in my seat, followed by his buddies. Mesmerized by his dazzling display of knifemanship, I just stood there dumfounded and started to feel a queasy mix of fear and anger in my gut. Then Eddie got in my ear and said, "You gonna let that guy do that to you?" I decided not, turned, and punched the knifeman alongside his head, which caused a wave of crashing bodies. He bounced off the wall, and they all jumped toward us. We knocked the railing down and landed on the floor in the middle of the bar. I found myself pinned down on my back under a mass of headlocks and ground fighting. A couple of badass bouncers quickly ripped the pile apart, got in my face and told me to leave. I tried to explain, quite loudly, that I lost my glasses and couldn't leave without them. They started explaining to me why they didn't care, while taking side positions to take me down and out, when Brian B. thankfully appeared with my glasses. I left the bar to cool down outside.

One of the knifeman's buddies came out and started talking shit. I didn't feel much like talking and told him to get his friend to come outside without his knife. He came out, pulled out his knife, and here we go again; he's whipping it back and forth and telling me what he's going to do to me. He kept talking, and I walked up and punched him in the nose, knocking him on his ass and causing him to drop the knife. He got up and came at me trying to get a one-legged take down. He was a wrestler after all, but he charged me holding his head down, so I stepped aside and landed a straight right to his temple, knocking him down alongside a car. I stunned him, grabbed his hair, and started banging his head against a hubcap. He slumped over onto his back but still fought to get up. That's when I turned into the Wolfman, pounced on him, bit a chunk of flesh from his chest and spit it out. He screamed and tried to scramble to his feet by turning onto all fours, but I pressed my body down heavy on his back; he fell down flat, and I tried to get him in a rear choke hold. That's when he tried to bite my finger off, which hurt like hell and ended the fight. I got off him, and he slumped onto his back, undone. His friends dragged him off, and I assumed they drove him to the hospital.

Then I received my trophy. Brian B. picked up the guy's knife after he dropped it. I later took pride showing it off while telling the story but never mastered the ability to flip it around like Bruce Lee. He received a special gift as well. One of his boys picked up my wallet after it fell out of my back pocket. It held my driver's license in it with my address. A couple of weeks later, he and his boys showed up looking for me. I wasn't home, but Dad managed to thoroughly intimidate them, and they left. Their only recourse was to later drive by and throw a rock through the living room window while my parents and younger brothers watched TV. It scared the shit out of them. A couple of my friends who partied at Salt's that night met the knifeman a few months later. He worked as a bouncer in a small bar in Smithtown. They talked about the fight. They described him as a nice enough guy. You had to be tough to be a bouncer, but I knew that only a cowardly punk needed a knife. I never saw him again. I never saw my wallet again either.

One positive note of my growing reputation; it provided an insurance policy for my siblings, especially my brothers. Nobody messed with them.

Like at Belshazzar's feast in The Book of Daniel, my parents saw the writing on the wall. They sat down with me one day and laid out their five-year plan: I had to leave the day after I turned 21. They would buy me a one-way ticket anywhere I wanted to go within the forty-eight contiguous states. I think the conversation started with Dad's prophetic word over my life, again, "Ray, you're going through The School of Hard Knocks and the way things are going for you, I see three things happening in your life: either you're going to jail, the nut house, or you're going to end up dead." We adhered to the plan and Dad's prophecy came true; I did time in jail, the nut house, and died to myself when I was born again in Christ.

As evidenced by Mom's Journal, toward the end of summer leading into my senior year I decided to get my shit together. Her journal entries from August 31, marking the start of football camp through the end of 1976, narrate my relatively quiet compliance with the rules during football season, both at home and at school. However, when inspired, I wrote a couple of responses myself, and a number of entries leading up to that point reflect Mom's dogged diligence and the meaningful exchanges between us. At times, Mom was at a loss for words, like on June 7, when she wrote, "Ray—suspended again —- what to write" On June 16, she noted that I "left @ 8 30 whereabouts unknown" to which I added that "only the SHADOW KNOWS!" upon returning that evening. For the sake of accuracy, after she entered that I "Came home by 10 30" I corrected the record to reflect that it was "BEFORE 10:30 like 9:45" The very next day, I tried to both promote myself and encourage Mom after she wrote "Did not go out" by declaring "(HURRAY!) We are spared a night of grief worrying about the mishaps in the life of this terrible boy!!! (What will he do next?) STAY TUNED AND FIND OUT!" Clearly a preview for my next entry on June 18, after Mom once again expressed the angst of not knowing my whereabouts and activities, and the small respite in knowing that I "Came home @ 1 45 A" when I wrote, "YES AT PARTY FOLKS AND WHAT A PARTY!! (RAY HAD NOTHING TO DRINK OR SMOKE TONIGHT BELIEVE IT OR NOT)" On July 8, Mom reported that she "Spoke to Ray again about late hours—no result? . . . seemed quite angry."

This next entry needs some explanation. There was an Italian cop in our neighborhood nicknamed "The Gray Ghost," because of the premature color of his hair and his ability to sneak up on people. We also called him "218," the number of his squad car. For some inexplicable reason, he didn't like me. But he did seem to enjoy harassing me by detaining me as often as possible for loitering on school grounds and taking me to my parents' house to discuss my ongoing criminality. The entry from July 9 provides some important facts about the day: "Ray up @ 11 00 / still angry about last night / Police & Bldg. Super. came to house @ 6 00 asking to see R.—seems someone wrote in 2ft. letters on L.A. school

'218 is a fuck'—thought it might be R. / Man did not recognize him—apologized / P.D. after R"

Mom knew The Ghost was after me. What she didn't know is that Tito vouched for me that day, telling The Ghost that I had been home the entire time. Tito and The Ghost both knew that I was the graffiti artist, and God's mercy covered me that day. The building superintendent drove right up on me as I finished the job and chased me on my bike. I raced around the back of the school and lost him by going down the field and back home via a circuitous route, something I excelled at as a result of prior experience. I returned home just in time to make it to the basement and freshen up a bit. I said a quick prayer and took off my glasses before going up in hopes of disguising my identity. It obviously worked; I let Mom believe it, and Tito and I never spoke about it. The look on The Ghost's face was remarkable!

Mom's journal documents my selfish, insensitive, disrespectful, and often times asinine conduct, such as on July 21 when she wrote, "Ray up w/ I PM / (think car ins 1.3 miles / no license — no permission) states just driving up and down driveway / 'What's the Big Deal?' I refused to drive him to work" And she *should* have refused to drive me after that lame story. Too much drinking and drugging had clearly destroyed a good number of brain cells. Mom's entries from July 30 and 31 are heartbreaking: "left @ 11 PM for a walk / 4 15 and not home / did not come home / did not call / 2 PM and still no word from Ray / Came home @ 3 10" August 29, 1976: "Dead drunk / Got sick during night and vomited all over room"

"This can be nothing but sadness of the heart."

NEHEMIAH 2:2

14

SENIOR YEAR

DURING MY LAST YEAR IN HIGH SCHOOL, I RAN AND LIFTED EVERY day. I also worked two jobs, as a busboy at Chirillo's Steakhouse in Smithtown and stock/sales in the lumber and hardware department at Modell's Shopper's World right down the street. I worked out on the job as well. At Modell's, I muscled up 200-pound metal sheds onto my shoulders, carried them out of the store and placed them in customer's cars. At Chirillo's, I prided myself on stacking the largest trays in restaurant history. One night, I attempted an unofficial world record. I cleared an entire party setting of twenty—plates, bowls, glasses, silverware, and tablecloths. The stack reached probably four feet high. I lifted it up to my shoulder with ease and steadily walked through the dining area toward the kitchen. I could see and sense the fear in the customers, whose eyes grew large as I passed their tables. I carried it confidently until I approached the swinging doors into the kitchen. It didn't clear at the top, and I went straight back and down, recording the unofficial largest tray wipeout in restaurant history. Amazingly, no one got hurt and I didn't get fired.

Football was crazy. I'd grown from 135 lbs., dripping wet, in ninth grade to 175 lbs. my senior year—and still fast in spite of all the drinking and drugging. It's amazing the abuse a teenage body can take. Before we left for camp, I ran a 4.7 forty in bare feet. A significant shift in the athletic order of things happened during the first week of camp. We always lined up for a tackling drill to end the day. We placed a bunch of tackling dummies on the ground, spaced about four feet apart. Half the team lined up on one end and half on the opposite end. A simple drill, one guy carried the ball along the line and attempted to cut through two of the dummies, while the other guy had to tackle him before he got through the space. I loved the violence. Things went along and I waited my turn. Fred stood in front of me. Fred was one of the nicest guys, and everybody loved him. He had guts, but as a short, pudgy kid with no speed, strength, or agility, he really served as the team manager in pads. He and Tony came up against each other, but before Fred got destroyed, I took the ball from him and stepped up to take on Tony. The entire team and all the coaches went wild. I could hit and tackle harder than anyone on the team (except for Eddie, who started at fullback and middle linebacker since our junior year), but Tony always had beat me, a shoestring from my grasp. A great athlete and one of the best running backs in the conference, he started on varsity as a sophomore and scored three touchdowns against South that year, while rushing for over 100 yards. But, partying hard for those years and doing a lot of coke slowed him down. He looked burned out. Here we go! Ray and Tony—mano a mano. Come on! Let's go! Tony started jogging down the line, looking to suddenly accelerate, fake me out and slash through the hole. Not today. We both broke at the same time. I charged in low and went straight threw him, driving him back about five yards before planting him in the ground, a perfect tackle. I didn't even feel the impact. The hit blew out Tony's knee and sidelined him for most of the season. Things changed in the world order.

During camp I made the decision to change positions. I played outside linebacker in a 4–3 defense, but we switched to a 3–4, and the coaches pumped up the nose guard position. You could play on all fours, a three-point stance, or standing up, and could shoot left or right after demolishing the center. But most importantly, the nose guard needed to be the toughest guy on the team, and I needed to be that player. I won the job. Only 175 lbs., which was light for the defensive line, I went up against guys that were 200 to 235. My speed and toughness got me through, but I got injured (sprained ankle) and essentially played on one leg by the end of the season. All my hard work resulted in being named captain of the defense. Our quarterback, John B., the captain of the offense, was an honor roll student, a straitlaced preppy on his way to college on a scholastic/academic scholarship. The night of the preseason pep rally highlighted our differences. John talked about our new offensive strategies and the hard work we put in. When he finished, he received a scattered few claps and shout-outs from the audience. I came to the microphone and let everyone know that the defense was badass—looking for blood—and everyone should come out to watch us crack some skulls. The gymnasium went crazy.

We sucked that year and ended up with a 4–6 record. Only a handful of seniors played on the team, and most of the underclassmen were soft. The defense worked hard, but our offense, a three-and-out shitshow, always kept us on the field. I think our punter set a league record for most punts that year. It all broke on me at an away game versus West Islip. They kicked our asses, 41 to 0. When I got on the bus after the game, I heard a bunch of the guys laughing and joking about the game being in the papers the next day. They didn't give a crap, and it really pissed me off. Without saying a word, I took off my helmet and started smashing it down on the heads of those idiots as I walked toward the back of the bus. Most of them still had their helmets on, and those that didn't quickly put them on before I passed by. With each blow I shouted out, "Let 'em put this in the paper!" The season wasn't a total waste. Because of all my playing time, I led the league with the most tackles for a defensive lineman (ninety-five) and made the All-Conference Team. I received the Most Improved Player award at the team banquet (which I hated, because I wanted best tackler), and Coach D. sent my highlight tape to a friend of his who coached at Hofstra University. He offered me a partial scholarship and an opportunity for a full ride if I performed on and off the field. Fat chance of that.

The devil didn't have to expend much effort in my direction in those days. I didn't need his help for self-destruction.

A loser at love, my problem: I loved too many and gave too much love. In my junior year, I dated a few girls, but none lasted more than a couple of months. Poetry and timing; I always possessed mad poetry skills. As a child, I wrote "Ode to a Bathtub," a haunting lament so full of sorrow that it almost persuaded my mother to relinquish me from my chore of cleaning the bathtub. I wrote love poems, like Shakespeare. But where Bill wrote poems to specific women, I wrote for all womenkind, giving my gift to all, like Jesus. The same gift. The same love poem. Such love produced some pain, as I realized one day while strolling through the cafeteria. I saw Carolyn, Eleanor, and Liz sitting at the same table, reading something together and staring at me as I passed by. They had a look of disgust on their faces, a pre-vomit nauseous kind of look. I wasn't insensitive to their pain, just a horny dog (like all guys). I kept trying. A lot of things happened in the cafeteria, like the day that Judy sat across from me, took off her shoe, placed her foot between my legs and pumped, hard.

In my senior year, I started dating a sophomore named Carol. Our very first time together she gave me a hand job. One night she gave me oral sex in her bedroom, but my growing excitement did wane a bit when she paused and expressed some worry that we might be discovered in the act. I spent a lot of time with Carol. Even though I worked at two jobs, I hadn't yet purchased a car because of spending all my money on weed, speed, and beer. Fortunately, she lived close by, and we walked back and forth between houses based on the opportunities presented.

But Mom worked the graveyard shift and mostly spent her time at home during the day. She didn't need to use her psychic powers to see the physical attraction and mandated that we vacate the premises when she left for the store or to run an errand. On one such occasion, we doubled back into my bedroom in the basement. Carol started the oral sex when Mom burst through the door and found us on the bed. She had doubled back on our double back and busted us. Carol ran out of the house, and I received the fateful

73

command, "Raymond! I don't care what you do out in the fields in the dirt, but you will not have sex in this house!" I stayed down in the basement for a long time. The idea that sex was sinful and dirty (thanks to the nuns at Christ the King) had been driven deep into my psyche. After Dad came home that night, I could hear my parents talking in the kitchen and climbed to the top of the stairs just in time to hear Mom say, "You should've seen him, Fred. He was erected to the ceiling." I'm sure this statement, which is very disturbing on multiple levels, led to the performance anxiety and premature ejaculation that plagued me during my future sexual endeavors, until being saved by my future wife, Paula, in a different place and time. God protected us through high school by keeping us apart and forgave me for placing her as the centerpiece of my masturbatory life, always in her cheerleading outfit. "Ray Lopez, FIGHT, FIGHT, he's gonna help us win tonight!"

After my junior year, they erected a twelve foot chain-link fence surrounding the entire school in response to all the drugs and graffiti. And narcs enrolled in classes during our senior year. Tony, the main dealer, moved a lot of weed and occasionally cocaine. His mobbed-up dad received numerous warnings from friendly cops, strongly advising that Tony cease and desist. He ignored them, and the day he turned eighteen that spring, they arrested him for selling to an undercover cop. Even though we competed as rivals, we had love and respect for each another. Hearing the news really pissed me off and upset everyone. The day we heard, a bunch of us were hanging out in front of the school, where there was an open field around the flagpole and a row of benches to sit on. Free for eighth period on a beautiful, cloudless spring day, we started tossing the Frisbee around. Mr. L. approached to remind us of the rule that during any free period, students were only allowed to go to the library, the cafeteria, or off school grounds. I tried to appeal to his better nature and said, "Come on Mr. L. It's a beautiful day. We're just playing Frisbee and waiting for school to get out (there were about ten minutes left in the period). Can't you just make an exception, just this one time?" He responded by taking out his warrant pad and began writing. To which I said, "Mr. L., why are you writing me up?" He replied, "For insubordination and failing to follow staff directions." "What?! Well if you're writing me up, I may as well call you a fucking asshole!" His eyes got bigger; he took a step back and continued to write furiously. I realized that he was writing down every word I said, so I decided to dictate a slew of obscenities for him as he kept writing and backing up. I didn't realize I was stepping toward him with each curse, but I did notice that his face kept getting redder, which inspired me to end my assault by telling him that he was a fucking pussy. Mr. L. had had enough; he turned and speed-walked into the school. Shortly thereafter, Mr. S. came out and escorted me to the vice principal's office. The vice principal, Mr. B., informed me that Mr. L. lodged an official complaint that I threatened to assault him.

They planned on reviewing my case before the Board of Education to determine whether or not I should be expelled for my conduct. I knew I had screwed myself and scared Mr. L. I angrily yelled and screamed at him, the kid who ripped the sink out of the bathroom wall, the kid who went through the glass window in the cafeteria, the kid who could break your neck. The decision didn't take long. The following Monday, they advised my parents of my expulsion and invited them to come in for a meeting to receive the paperwork and discuss the circumstances. Mom decided not to attend and started preaching consequential thinking: you've made your own bed and now you can lay in it. But surprisingly, Dad went to the meeting, and to this day, I don't know what he said. All I know is that he came home and told me I was no longer expelled but had been suspended for one month until the end of the school year. I had to complete my assignments and mail them in, and the last time I would ever be allowed back on school grounds was to take my final exams. That meant that I couldn't attend the graduation ceremony. I couldn't believe it. This was the best thing that had ever happened to me. I get a month vacation and I get to graduate. But following my joy was a separate price to pay. When Coach D. heard what happened, he got angry, called his friend at Hofstra, told him the story and said that I had an attitude problem. I lost the scholarship offer. I did have another opportunity that summer after I made the Long Island North Shore All-Star Team as a linebacker. After practicing for two weeks we played the South Shore team on a Friday night at Central Islip. There were coaches and recruiters from all the major Northeast colleges and universities in the stands. To get an edge I took two white 697s before the game and ran around the field during the first half like a chicken with its head cut off without making a single tackle. Nobody was impressed with that shit show and I did not receive another offer.

The lifetime ban from Commack North was withdrawn a few years later. Trying to get my shit together, I convinced the health teacher that I was in recovery and wanted to share my experience as a warning to others. I did sincerely want to help people (though I was still partying). They allowed me back on school grounds for one day as a guest speaker in the health classes. I started my talk by referencing the display case of drugs that "Officer Friendly" brought in each year to tell us of the evils of narcotics, hallucinogens, and stimulants. Then I pounded my chest and said, "This is *my* display case!" Years later I learned that my future brother-in-law, Jon, cut classes to hear me speak.

I'm grabbing Tony's chest and Pat D is wearing sunglasses and suspenders.

"The fear of the Lord is the beginning of knowledge but fools despise wisdom and instruction."

PROVERBS 1:7

15

ADDITIONAL CRIMINAL HISTORY

SHORTLY AFTER GRADUATING FROM HIGH SCHOOL, I GOT ARrested again. Early one morning on July 9, 1977, we stopped at the Jack in the Box in Commack on Jericho Turnpike after a long night of partying into morning. Everybody went there to end the night, and some went to find a fight. One could always find another drunken fool looking for the same thing, trying to prove his manhood to nobody cares. Consequently, they hired some badass security guard to try to keep the damage to a minimum. We ordered food, sat down, and became so loud, the guard told us to leave. He held the door for us, and as we stumbled out, I noticed he placed his hand on his nightstick. I didn't appreciate that. We were cooperating and leaving, and I felt his posture to be a bit excessive. In my altered state, I actually thought for a moment on how to respond to my feelings and subsequently grabbed his nightstick, asking, "What are you going to do with this?" He answered with a fist to my face and knocked me on my back. I guess I expected a quick surrender to my dominance, followed by an apology and polite request for the return of his stick. My buddies quickly helped me to my feet, and we tore into each other, exchanging blows to the face. He could fight, but I eventually beat him down to his knees.

At that point, I realized that he held my belt, determined to detain me until the Fourth Precinct's finest arrived.

Completely gassed, I didn't have the strength to break his grip. I escaped by unbuckling my belt, jumping in my old station wagon and driving home without my glasses, once again lost during a fight. When I pulled onto my street, I saw three squad cars in front of the house, lights flashing. I turned the headlights off, pulled into a driveway, got out, and ducked behind some bushes on the side of a neighbor's house. The cops saw my car and started driving up and down the block and around the corner, shining searchlights everywhere. I used my evasive skills and managed to make it home by running through backyards and crawling under bushes and light beams. I ran into the backyard, stripped down to my underwear and went in the pool. All sweaty and muddy, looking like an inmate from *Cool Hand Luke*, I needed to cool down. I thought I could use the alibi that I was swimming all night practicing the backstroke and that it must be a case of mistaken identity.

Before I could make it to the deep end, several of the Fourth Precinct's finest surrounded the pool while my mom and siblings stood by. They didn't buy my story, told me I was under arrest for assault and ordered me out of the pool. Mom yelled at me, "Raymond! Get out of the pool!" I told the cops the water felt fine and they should just cool down. For emphasis, I playfully splashed them from the middle of the shallow end. Matt the Cop, all 6'5" of him, took a step closer and said, "If I have to come in and get you, it's going to be an electrifying experience." I almost started laughing because I thought it such a stupid thing to say, but the cool water sobered me up. I regained some semblance of my senses and got out of the pool. They started to cuff me in my underwear and take me down, but Mom persuaded them to let me put on a pair of pants. All the cops knew her from the ER and had much love and respect for her, which came back to me on occasion. The DA dropped the charges, so the only real consequence I suffered was taking shit from my buddies because this guy knocked me on my ass and pinned me down, leaving scrapes on my back. A few years later, Paula told me she met the guy up at SUNY in Oswego, when she visited her friend, Kim. He was also a student there, and they met at a party. They noticed a big scar above his eye and asked how he got it. He told them he fought a crazy guy named Ray Lopez when working as a security guard at Jack in the Box. An all-state wrestler in high school, he also wrestled at Oswego. He knew wrestling, but I knew crazy.

"Be sober, be vigilant; because your enemy the devil walks about like a roaring lion, seeking whom he may devour."

1 PETER 5:8

16

MESSING WITH THE MOB

We loved Carmela's. It was our favorite place and one of the best pizza restaurants on the Island. It was also mobbed up. The owner was a member of the Gambino family, and every Friday and Saturday night, you'd see the black Lincoln Continentals parked on the side. The racist chefs came straight out of Sicily. Hanging out front one night, I went inside to order a slice while they were closing. A couple of the chefs at the counter started stacking pizza boxes while the fat guys in suits sat in the back room smoking cigars and drinking shots. While heating up my slice, the chefs started talking about waiting for the spic to come in to mop the floors and clean the shit out of the bathrooms. They laughed and kept looking at me while talking about the spic cleaning the shit. I quickly boiled over, told them to fuck the slice and come outside to fight me. I went out and stood in front of the window and kept yelling at them to come out so I could kick their asses. They clearly didn't want to fight and tried ignoring me, which made me angrier. I kicked the front window, shattering it. Within seconds, all the chefs and suits spilled out onto the sidewalk. The chefs armed themselves with knives and pizza boards. My friends got in front of me while everyone was shouting, and I was still calling out the chefs. Eddie got in my ear and told me I should get out of there, which suddenly made total sense. I jumped in my sister's car, a big station wagon, and accidently slammed it into drive. Her car crashed over the curb; I slammed it into reverse and drove away. The next night I worked at Chirillo's. Mr. C. called me into his office, told me he heard about Carmela's and asked if I had any family down south where I could go until things cooled down. He told me that either way, I should lay low, take some time off, and stay away from Carmela's.

I followed his advice for the next couple of weeks, but one night I was with Eddie and Lenny in Eddie's muscled Road Runner, when they decided they needed to get a slice at Carmela's. After smoking a few joints, the munchies overrode any concern for my safety. But we all agreed that I should stay in the back seat. They came out carrying the pizza and were leaning against the car, eating and talking to some girls, when Mr. Gambino stepped out and asked, "Where's your buddy who broke my window?" A short, lean, middle-aged man with streaks of grey hair above his ears, he wore a white collared shirt and suspenders. Tired of hiding, I shifted into crazy, got out of the car and said, "Here I am." He walked up to me and said, "You know, Lopez, I could've had my guys grab you a dozen times. But I like you kids coming around." Then, he softly patted my left cheek, gave it a hard pinch and said, "Just don't break my window again." I became aware of nodding my head up and down in affirmation, and when he went back inside, I started breathing again.

After I turned 18 that fall, I started working as a bouncer at Lucifer's. We'd been drinking there for about a year using phony IDs. Photo licenses didn't exist in New York at the time, and you just needed to be prepared to answer two questions: what's your date of birth, and how old are you? The two bouncers, Adam and Tiny, members of The Pagans, an outlaw biker gang, both stood well over six-feet tall. We had seen Adam knock guys out with one punch. Tiny weighed about 400 pounds; he could practically suffocate a guy by pinning him against the wall. Other gang members occasionally frequented the joint, which made for a volatile mix. The owner, Kotter, needed someone quick on his feet and a bit more diplomatic than the bikers. I convinced him to hire me because I could beat up all my friends, and they listened to me.

A lot of action took place at Lucifer's, like when a Pagan harassed my sister out front and I pushed him across the hood of a car. He went home to allegedly get his shotgun but never came back, thank you, Jesus. On another early morning ending at Lucifer's, my sister agreed to give Eddie and Brian R. a ride home. Teresa and I were in the front seat singing along to *Black Betty* on her 8-Track player (*Whoa, Black Betty Bam-Ba-Lam, Whoa, Black Betty Bam-Ba-Lam*) when I noticed that my boys were passed out and cuddling in the back seat. I pointed it out to her and we started laughing hysterically causing Teresa to sway and hit a parked car, rendering her vehicle inoperable. A cop arrived shortly thereafter. Fortunately he knew me and he knew our Mom from the ER and decided to help us out without giving Teresa a sobriety test or a ticket. Eddie decided to walk to his girlfriend's house as she lived nearby and the cop offered to drive Brian home after calling for a tow truck. He had to wait for the truck to arrive. Brian got impatient and asked the cop if he was going to "give him a fucking ride home or what?" The cop said "With that attitude you can walk!" and as he turned to walk to his car, Brian ran up and punched him in the back of the head! What a crazy asshole! Brian was placed under arrest and the cop decided to search Teresa's car. He found some marijuana seeds and gave her a ticket for possession. She ended up going to court and paid a fine.

Tony hadn't gone to prison yet, and one night at Lucifer's some kid from The Bronx, a cousin of one of the guys from South, slashed open Tony's forearm with a switchblade. After high school, North and South agreed to vent our anger through weekend games of tackle football—no equipment, of course. Vigorous competition often resulted in concussions and broken bones, and occasionally for show and tell, someone retaliated by grabbing a gun from the trunk of a car, but nobody got shot. We matured enough to get through the slashing incident and never saw the Bronx kid again. Tony spent about three years at Elmira State Prison. We wrote each other, and I visited a few times. About a decade later, when

Paula and I were in California, my brother-in-law sent us an article about Tony catching the winning touchdown pass in the Long Island Flag Football League Championship. I felt good for him. But soon after, we learned that he died from a heroin overdose.

> "'Meaningless! Meaningless!" says the Teacher. "Utterly Meaningless!
> Everything is Meaningless."
>
> ECCLESIASTES 1:2

17

ON A SPIRITUAL PLANE

I STILL PURSUED POWER, BUT MY DESIRE ELEVATED TO A SPIRI-
tual plane to complement my physicality. I read books on astral
projection and telepathy, achieving some modest success yet un-
aware of the satanic forces at work. I read about those able to leave
their bodies and attend celestial classes where they learned of the
deeper functioning of the mind and the universe. My projections
turned mostly horrific. I always started by laying down, getting
still, and meditating on my breath, followed by a buzzing sound;
then, a catatonic seizure, like an elephant sitting on my chest; then,
a falling down out of my body onto the floor or under the bed
or into a dark place. A state of sheer panic ensued, which always
shot me back into my body, hyperventilating and sweating. I read
about people hovering above their own bodies before taking off
on a magical mystery tour. I guess I made some progress because
I kept trying regardless of the horror. One night, while alone in
the house watching TV in the family room, I found myself hovering just below the ceiling, which looked like an alien landscape
covered with crystal formations illuminated by TV moonlight. I
watched Johnny Carson but felt terrified to look down at my body,
afraid I would die if I saw myself.

I practiced my telepathic skills with impressionable young ladies. I somehow found myself attending the Lutheran church down the street, really just attracted to Mrs. O., one of my mom's friends, and a member of the church. I joined the choir to meet girls and found out that I could sing. I started seeing two choirgirls, both going into their senior year in high school. They came under my charm through my good looks, my voice, and my passion for things like telepathy, which doesn't work on everyone—only those psychically connected. Cindy and I connected, and I taught her how to train her mind to picture a blank white screen or sheet, to open her mind and concentrate only on her breathing. We designated a time, usually early in the morning, like 3:00 a.m., when most slept in the darkness and silence. We trained to take captive every thought to make it obedient and vanish into the white screen, and I projected a number or an image onto the screen. It required faith and persistence. I started sending and she started receiving, first numbers, then colors. Cindy started freaking out, and her parents became greatly concerned after she told them that I meditated on the full moon. I stopped seeing her and stopped practicing telepathy for the moment. Instead, I started reading everything I could find about psychokinetic powers.

The animosity between Commack North and South still existed. Although we all pretty much knew each other and tried to work it out by playing tackle football without pads, the possibility of rogues getting shitfaced and going on a search-and-seizure mission remained. This involved driving around on the other side of town trying to find somebody to jump. They almost got me one morning. Drinking and smoking weed all night at Silo Park, I passed out and woke up around 3:00 in the morning on a bench in the dugout. I guess my friends didn't notice or didn't want to disturb my sleep, so I started the two-and-a-half-mile walk home. About halfway up Burr Road, a carload of guys passed me, shut the headlights off, turned around and headed back. I took off down a side street and climbed into a friend's treehouse in the woods on the side of his house. They turned onto the street, stopped, got out of the car and started looking around. I stayed put and tried to calm down and steady my nerves. My heart pounded; adrenaline pumped. They got back into their car and slowly drove up the street. I planned to make it to the woods that led to the cornfield behind Bishop McDonald Camp where I could wait it out or sprint home if it was safe. I cautiously made my way, block by block, keeping a lookout for my pursuers, hiding behind bushes and parked cars, running when they were out of sight. It took forever, but I eventually made it home, sweaty and dirty and mad and scared. They drove down all the streets I would've traveled. I thought they might have marked me and knew where I lived. I wanted to be ready if they came. I didn't want another rock coming through my parents' living room window, so I grabbed a butcher knife from the kitchen and sat on the front steps until the break of dawn. They never came, thank God.

My journey to the center of self-destruction started picking up pace, as each night provided an opportunity to make great strides in that direction. During one night of bar hopping, me, Mike, Eddie and Brian R. drove the circuit looking to close a place down. Mike was driving. We pulled into People's Pub, hoping to catch last call. No luck. The bartender was wiping down the bar, and the place was empty. It must have been four in the morning. Mike, a 6'4," 250-pound professional boxer, really wanted a drink. We all did. We began loudly voicing our collective desire to the barkeep, when our attention was drawn to the sound of a double-barreled shotgun being cocked and ready to fire. The owner stepped out from the back room and started across the floor in our direction, telling us to "get the fuck out or I'm going to blow your fucking heads off." He kept moving toward us repeating himself, getting louder as he got closer. We started backing away, but everything was slow and heavy for me, like having an out-of-body experience. The owner and the bartender seemed really scared. The owner aimed his shotgun at us, holding his finger on the trigger, his eyes bugging out of his head. We backed out of the bar, never turning our backs on him. Innately, I knew you never turn your back on someone pointing a shotgun at you at close range. He followed us out and kept the gun pointed at us while delivery trucks began pulling into the parking lot to unload bread. We got in the car and traversed through an insanely tight space. Mike backed up between two trucks, leaving only inches to clear, slamming the gas pedal and burning rubber as we pulled onto Jericho Turnpike. Mike was a great driver, especially when wasted.

But you can only drive as far as the road will take you, and sometimes you can't turn around. I don't remember much else about that night, but I do remember the robbery at dawn on July 16, 1978. Six of us headed for the sunrise at King's Point Bluff. Mike was driving again, with Eddie and Mandy in front and Brian R., Cheryl, and me in the back. We pulled into a 7-11; the girls stayed in the car. We wanted a case of beer. The lone cashier, an Indian guy, told us he couldn't sell any alcohol on Sunday until noon because of the state law. Now I'd seen Brian snap before. His father, a mean drunk, used to beat the crap out of him at least once a week when Brian was a kid, leaving him ready to explode at any moment. He tried to appeal to the cashier's good nature in the spirit of adventure, but he went into the broken record technique: "I'm sorry, but I can't sell alcohol on Sunday until noon. It's state law." Brian came back with, "Come on man. It's a beautiful day. We're going to the beach. We've got the girls waiting in the car. . ." "I'm sorry, but I can't sell alcohol on Sunday until noon. It's state law." "Come on man. You've got to be kidding me." As the cashier went into his schpiel again, Brian yelled, "Fuck this!" and pulled out a switchblade. He tried to jump over the counter, but Eddie and Mike grabbed him. They all crashed to the floor, knocking over a display of Twinkies. And it was on! Brian started jumping around like a mad kangaroo while Eddie and Mike were trying to talk him down, shuffling laterally to block his repeated charges at the counter. During the action, I grabbed a case of Coronas, ran out the door and put the beer in the trunk. Right behind me, Mike and Eddie came out dragging and pushing Brian toward the car. We burned rubber out of there but decided to abort the beach trip. The King's Park Police Station was right around the corner, and within a minute, a squad car came up behind us. I felt the speed in my gut as we raced down residential streets, siren wailing close behind, houses and trees a blur, bodies leaning left and right with each screeching turn until, oh shit, we were at a dead end . . . and the chase ended.

The cop jumped out of his car, weapon drawn. Nobody moved. He came up on us shouting in a weird high-pitched tone, quivering, like it was hard for him to breathe, like he was scared. "Get the fuck out of the car and on the ground now!" We started to comply, and he screamed, "Hands up, motherfuckers!" Like we were in a movie. All the guys got out of the car, but for me, it was like slow motion again, moving underwater. The cop was alone; he was young, blond-haired, blue-eyed, probably a rookie. "Get down on the ground! On your faces, fuckers. Now!" We got down but the girls stayed in the car. Keeping his gun on us in his right hand, he reached into the car and pulled Mandy out by her hair. Cheryl fell out after her. We all sprawled out across someone's front lawn.

I smelled the fresh-cut grass and the flowers; I heard birds singing, heard him call for backup, and felt the crazy fear in the forefront of my mind, folding time again. I turned because I needed to look. I propped myself up on my right elbow and saw the barrel of his gun extending from my forehead to the handle in his hand, finger tight on the trigger. I felt the steel pressing further into my skull; his whole body was shaking, beads of sweat rolling down his face, with the gigantic pupils of his blue eyes surrounded by white circles. I couldn't move. The muscles in my neck stiffened like steel rods, and he started screaming again, but his voice got even higher. "Eat the fucking dirt, motherfucker, or I'll blow your head off, motherfucker!" I watched his finger on the trigger as the iron rods in my neck stiffened further. I knew if I moved, I was dead. Then I heard sirens sound of mercy and the cops, like angels from Heaven: "Stay down, spread your legs, and place your hands behind your back." The earth finally stopped shaking. He lowered his gun and slumped down to his knees, right beside me, head hanging down, sucking in deep, gasping breaths. We both started crying, and that fresh-cut grass never smelled so good. Brian received an armed robbery charge. I don't know about the others, but I pled guilty to harassment and received a conditional discharge plus a $100 fine. It was a good deal. Years later, I learned that Brian ended up doing some long stretches in prison, and was shot and killed in his early 50s.

Me with Brian R. holding the football.

"Therefore God has mercy on whom he wants to have mercy, and he hardens whom he wants to harden."

ROMANS 9:18

18

FAMILY MATTERS

My maternal grandparents moved to Little Havana in the 1970s. My grandmother, Aurelia, died on May 23, 1974, at the age of 70. Thereafter, my grandfather, Benigno (Tito), moved in with our family in Commack.

"Tito, Mi Abuelo"
You said your black beans were the best
this side of Heaven.
They were spicy
but your words made them go down easy.
Every night I raced through supper
till you raised my hands,
"The winner, number one
president of the clean plate club!

You said I was the best ballplayer
this side of heaven,
that I hit like Mantle and ran like Mays.

When one of us cried,
you'd hold a glass up to our eyes
and beckon us to fill it
with our tears until we laughed.

You made us all feel

that here with you,
this side of Heaven
was the best place to be.

Camel Straights
dragged the joy out of you, leaving
you wheezing through
one emphysema lung.
I carried you, ninety-five pounds,
and your oxygen tank,
to the car, to the doctor, to the car,
to the house and again,
tomorrow and tomorrow and tomorrow.

We raced to the finish line.
I was a blur on the streets.
White speed velocity so strong
I wouldn't have to feel the end.
You stayed in bed
at the far end of the house.

I had only planned to make a pit-stop
that night looking for food and money,
but you drew me in with your voice.
The chill in your room was thick
under the hot August moon,
the dog growling under your bed.
You breathed in, closer,
And whispered
Mary.
Wheeze
Mary
Wheeze
Mary

Mom wake up.
It's Tito.
He's calling you.
Mom I can't stay.

July 27, 1978: The house was hot and humid that early morning, no central air. My parents used a window air conditioning unit

for their room, and the rest of the house relied on the attic fan to pull in the cool air from outside. But the temperature read eighty degrees that night, and walking into Tito's room was like walking into a freezer. I could see my breath. The dog was growling, and he was dying. I left after waking up my Mom. But I slept in his bed the next night. I needed to. The Hispanic chapter of the Oddfellows gave him a Cuban wake with shots of Scotch whiskey. I would see him again, very soon. He would wake me up.

I was burning out, but if I got hold of some speed and weed, I could fly right into the night, into day, into night, and on and on and on until coming in for a crash landing, like one early morning in my parents' backyard. The animal in me again, just like that night at Salt's Pub, but with no one to fight, no one to bite, it seemed like a good idea at the time to eat grass and run head on into the trunk of the big oak tree in the back yard—several times—until I gassed out, almost passed out, and my father came out the back door to carry me in:

"Of the Father and the Son"

Too much
Mixing controlled
Substances
Premature
Expulsion
Immaculate Guilt

Full contact
Un-padded pressure
Loco motion
Sleepless distance,
Making Time
Fold into rage.

Another sunrise
And nothing left
But to ram himself
Into the tree.

He growls and eats the grass.
His Abuela prays

Every day in the name
Of the Father,
Who comes out
In nothing but his white
Fruit of the Looms

And the Son,
He fireman carries
Into the house
Because of himself,
The grass and the tree

Not the rest
Of the world
Which is what the Son feels
Believes
Not the weight of the world,
But the strength of his father's back
And the rest he feels
On his shoulders.

And so it goes. Close to the edge, what pushed me over was sex on a regular basis. Cheryl, a wild and beautiful brown-eyed beauty with auburn hair, shared my love of speed and could keep up with me. A little bit criminal and very dangerous, she was Mike's ex-girlfriend, but nothing else mattered. It was real, and I was ready to go the distance with Mike one night in a parking lot outside another pub, but once again God's mercy spared me. I was there with Cheryl and Eddie and Brian R. and who knows who when Mike showed up looking for blood. My buddies held me back while trying to talk some sense into me to keep me out of the hospital. Cheryl spoke to Mike, and by some miracle, calmed him down and led him to accept that it was over for them. And so it goes.

My sister didn't like Cheryl. She knew she was a bad girl who was going to hurt me. She was right, and her concerns were confirmed one night, literally, at the Twilight Zone (the Larkfield Pub), when she walked into the ladies' room to find Cheryl trying to pierce my ear, using a safety pin and an ice cube. With a look of disgust on her face, Teresa just turned and walked out. Both of us totally wasted, ice melted away, I told Cheryl to just push the pin through and almost passed out. She pierced my right ear, which customarily meant you were gay. My buddies thoroughly enjoyed my dilemma, but the piercing of my left ear occurred in Cheryl's kitchen under safe and sober conditions. Dad told me it was effeminate.

My sister didn't deal big time, but she always purchased good weed and sold to her friends to pay for her head. We once took a road trip together to Miami, where she copped a pound from her ex-boyfriend. One sex-filled, starry night into morning, I woke my sister up, looking for some free weed. She knew I was with Cheryl and told me where to go. I got pissed, exploded from the house, jumped into Cheryl's car and proceeded to peel out, in reverse, side-swiping my sister's car. There was damage done to both cars . . . and both relationships.

Perhaps Cheryl used me to hurt Mike, or she just liked getting wasted and having sex and didn't really mean to hurt me when she slept with Brian R. I saw her car parked outside his house that day and stopped and kicked and punched her car, doing who knows how much damage, but it felt good and right and my fists were hard. I toughened them many nights by punching concrete walls. Cheryl ended up suing me in civil court and showed up on judgment day with Mike. My parents gave me $500 for the restitution.

"Do not lust in your heart after her beauty or let her captivate you with her eyes."

PROVERBS 6:25

19

ON BECOMING CHRIST

On July 31, 1978, three days after the death of my grand-father, *TIME Magazine* published its cover story, "The First Test-Tube Baby," and God spoke to me. This was the anti-Christ, even if it was a she. The Bible set forth falsehood, and I would be called to set the record straight.

I arrived at South Oaks Hospital in Amityville, New York, in August of 1978. I assumed there to be some link between the hospital and the Amityville Horror house; maybe Ronald DeFeo Jr. had been a patient there. I don't know, but I knew evil lurked around the corner—and *He* wanted me to go there. My voice still spoke to the Universe, but I kept that to myself, as people weren't ready to receive it. Mom and Dr. R. assured me of my voluntary resident status, allowing me to leave any time, but they conspired against me; they lied. When asked what they liked about their son, my parents could only offer that "he worked hard at building his muscles and a strong body."

They locked me up in the adolescent ward and wanted to give me drugs, which I found ironic because of all the drugs I already used. And I knew that Dr. R., an overweight, sweaty Italian guy who smoked cigarettes, was some kind of Freudian freak, because he kept asking me if I had sexual fantasies about my mother, searching for some Oedipus Complex. I knew that he fantasized about my mother, and by projecting onto me, hoped that I did and would describe mine in detail, so he could get off. I was smarter than Dr. R. I was smarter than everyone in the World, the Universe.

But Dr. R. showed me the magic. We sat together in the interview room on the ward. While rock music played on the radio, he told me that I had manic depression with schizoid features, which I liked the sound of because Hendrix sang about manic depression, and I loved Hendrix. Dr. R. kept smoking the whole time, and the music kept playing; I don't remember the song, so let's just say it was "Manic Depression." As smoke swirled in the air, he asked, "Do you believe in magic?" Yes. I said yes, and before I could say anything more, he pulled out a pink pill called Lithium and proclaimed, "This is magic. Watch, I'll show you." And he pulled out a cigarette and placed it on the table between us and started circling his finger around it, clockwise and counter clockwise, fast and faster; and then he stopped, placed his finger on my side of the table near the cigarette and slowly dragged his finger toward me—but nothing happened. So he picked it up, lit it using his lighter, took a drag, blew out three perfect smoke rings and said, "This is just a cigarette. It's not magic." Then, he held up the pink pill and said, "But *this* is magic." He laid the pill down at the center of the table, smoke swirling, music playing, and began to make circles around the pill until he stopped and placed his finger on my side of the pill. When he moved his finger toward me, the pill followed and rolled in my direction until it was almost off the edge. It suddenly stopped, and he said, "You see, it's magic," and then handed me a glass of water. I swallowed the magic and knew his power, but knew he still couldn't be trusted.

After I started taking the magic Lithium, I became more powerful. I no longer needed to sleep, and although my telekinetic power limited me to picking numbers out of people's heads, I expanded to between one and twenty, achieving a 100-percent success rate. I knew I needed more practice. This excited my followers, the other kids on the ward, but the staff seemed just a little bit worried. I also began exploring my psychokinetic powers. Nothing major, just opening drawers an inch or so in my room in the presence of selected followers.

They gave me Thorazine to slow me down and something else to help me sleep. But I didn't sleep, as my mind evolved. The Thorazine affected my depth perception, making it hard to catch a fly ball in the outfield, but not my strength; after I hit the eighty-pound punching bag so hard that it smashed the lighting fixture in the ceiling, I knew they were scared of me. God gave me twelve wardmates, both male and female. Like the twelve tribes of Israel and the twelve disciples of Jesus, there was no coincidence—numerology plain and simple—and I began running numbers in my mind and looking for the signs. Evil lurked in the darkness, and the truth waited to be found in the light.

The devil tried to tempt me, like he did to Jesus. God placed a beautiful nurse on the ward, Maria, a Latina with dark brown eyes, black hair, and milky brown skin. A voluptuous, full-figured woman, she seduced me and I weakened. And although I never fantasized about my mother—much to Dr. R.'s disappointment—I loved nurses and fantasized about Maria; she knew it, and that fantasy came close to becoming true one day in my room. She came in, closed the door behind her and began to counsel me. When she asked what I wanted to get out of the program, I told her I wanted to go into the closet with her to explore her dark mysteries. Weakened, I started falling back into the shadows, and when she agreed to go into the closet and close the door, I felt the fear and ran from the room, barely surviving the attack. I knew I needed to stay pure in my new body, my evolving heart.

The truth came for me in my room early one morning. I always kept vigil during the witching hour, between 3:00 and 4:00 a.m. My roommate, Richie, a skinny 14-year-old white kid with acne, slept in his bed along the wall to the right of the door. Forming a right angle, my bed was along the wall on the right. The bathroom and closets were on the left side of the room. The concrete walls stood to defy any displacement of anger. Awake, I sat on the edge of my bed, thinking about numbers and the new math I was creating. I looked at the digital clock on my night table and saw that it flashed 3:19, when Richie went into a violent seizure, convulsions. I watched his body twist and turn, getting wrapped up in the sheets like a snake coiling around him, around his neck, choking him. In that moment, I knew my calling, the beginning of the rest of my life. I boldly called out to the demon within him, "Come after *me*! I'm the one you want, not this boy!" Richie suddenly stopped cold—frozen—and said, "Death," not in his own voice but an ancient one, like rumbling bowels, raspy and croaking and deep, and I feared I might die. A foul smell filled the room, like piles of fresh, hot defecation; I buried my face in my pillow, laying prostrate. Then I heard the voices of many demons, whiny and high pitched, speaking in alien tongues; Then I heard the sound of scratching on the wall to the side of my bed. The scratching stopped, and I felt a powerful force grab my right triceps; I couldn't move my arm, and the force grew stronger, like a vice. I wanted to live, and I cried out in my heart and in my soul—like Jonah in the belly of the giant fish at the bottom of the sea—for God to help me, and I felt his strength. I began to lift my arm, slowly at first, then faster, until I threw the demons off. I turned and sat up to face the enemy, only to find Richie sitting calmly in his bed, watching me. And I smelled flowers in the room and saw sparkles in the air, and I knew I was the Savior, the Christ the people waited for, but not in the image imprinted on their minds by man. I asked Richie if he felt ok and to tell me what happened to him. He described, in detail, having a terrible nightmare in which a demon, like a dragon man, attacked him, pinned him down and was choking him, and he just woke up and thought he smelled flowers. I told him what really happened, and we looked and saw the deep scratches on the wall, traveling a path from the head of his bed to mine.

The night staff barely acknowledged me when I walked out of the room. I never slept and always came out in the early morning to talk or read. They didn't see the flames of the Holy Spirit in the windows of each room I passed, but they did see when the three young women on the ward came out of their rooms and hugged me without saying a word, before being ushered back to their rooms. And the staff paid no attention when I filled the blackboard, furiously, My Father God using automatic writing, creating the new math, the new symbols, the Neo-New Testament. They would have to know—the world *needed* to know—and I knew the Saturday morning group session at 11:00 provided the perfect moment for me to announce my arrival. Before group, my sister came to visit me and have breakfast. After we ate, I told her about defeating the demons, then took her to my room and showed her the scratches on the wall.

We sat in our group circle. The angry one sat directly across from me; my betrayer, my Judas, although his name was Peter. He was short, ghostly white, with a small, tangled mop of black hair and thick eyebrows. He knew my real identity and God's plan for my life. The demons I had cast out of Richie joined the demon already in him, and they tried to distract me through his dark eyes, but they didn't have the power and authority. I took Peter out before they could speak and lie to the others, trying to turn them against me, and the sharing went clockwise in his direction. He leaned back in his chair, like he always did, wearing that arrogant smirk on his face. I had practiced my psychokinetic powers, and now the time to perform had arrived. I closed my eyes and projected an image onto the blank white screen in my mind. Suddenly, his chair swept out from beneath him, rapidly dropping him back, his head banging off the hard floor; he was unconscious for a moment, speechless, concussed with a glazed-over look in his eyes as he was wheeled out of the ward on the way to the medical unit. I saw it all on the screen and released this misfortune upon him—his flesh, his mind's eye—and heard the sound of his head cracking the floor before I opened my eyes to see.

After they removed Peter from the ward, the group continued and I waited for my turn to speak. When it came, I rose before them, walked over to the blackboard and announced that "I am the Christ, the true Christ!" I pointed to the board and proclaimed, "This is this, the True New Testament, the Word as it is written by me!"

My followers gathered 'round, asked many questions, and desired to learn more, but the staff acted quickly; within the hour, they took me to the Chronic Ward. I went peacefully, as I knew my Lord meant for me to go. Things moved quickly after that, in the folded time that I created to teach the world. Simple, in the new math, time gets folded day by day, hour after hour, month by month, into years—like a neatly folded blanket—until God unfolds it and stretches time out to irrationality, eternity, and begins folding time again; in my time, the unfolding time, in the time of the speed of the snap of the blanket when God shakes it out. Speed, pure speed, like it had always been for me, speed, like The Flash.

As I stood at the nurses' station receiving my orientation, I noticed the fragile woman standing behind me, well under five feet tall, thin to the bone and not quite as white as her robe. She had beautiful, long blonde hair, straight and shiny, hanging down past her shoulders. Bent forward, her hair covered half her face. Crunched over like a hunchback, leaning to the right, she rocked back and forth, back and forth, back and forth, her right leg back, her left slightly forward, back and forth. I could see the peace in her heart, and I knew that although deaf and dumb, she knew she could speak to me and that I could hear her heart, if only she could touch my bathrobe; but her time was folding, back and forth, and she had miles to go before she could sleep. When the enemy came into the room, as another new patient, he came as a beautiful African Princess, an elegant young woman with dark brown skin, sparkling green eyes, long, lean muscular legs, and a face that could launch a thousand ships. Escorted by a nurse on each side of her, gently holding her arms, she saw me; the moment the Princess looked into my eyes, she screamed "Lucifer! Lucifer!" Then she broke free, turned, and punched the small blonde woman with a straight right to her left temple, dropping her to the ground, crumbling into that false sleep, clouded in darkness. The nurses regained control, took her down to the ground. They straddled her legs and firmly held her arms, while a third nurse came and injected their sleep serum into her arm and dragged her away. Then they took the rocking woman away on a stretcher, being very careful with her neck. Again, I was tempted.

The old fear came upon me. I found myself sunken in the flesh, and I knew I wanted to hit someone and hurt someone; then, I received God's way to stand up from under it. Easy. I told one of the male nurses, a big, burly, bearded black guy, that I felt like hurting someone. "No worries," he said, "we have something that can help you with that." And they shot me in the ass with a long needle that held a drug that buried time.

I still couldn't sleep, and now I couldn't move. They placed me in a room where others buried under time wrestled their own demons. I laid on my back at an upward angle, so I didn't choke on the constant drool dripping down my chin. My mind, slowed by the drug, rendered me unable to save the man beside me who wrestled the demons of his addiction, withdrawing their love from his veins in cold agony between hot and cold, daybreak and the deepest night. And I watched the lights over the parking lot that I could see from my bed. I waited for the end of each day, drooling, breathing in the rhythm of Heaven, until the sun went down enough and the lights came on. When the sun rose again and the lights went out, I knew I was living death . . . to descend into Hell until rising again. And I rose again. Finally, unfolding time like my heavenly father, I stood up from under that heavy blanket of deception and walked out of that room, as if walking through a deep mist into the light, back to myself.

My parents were amazed at my return to Earth. The experts told them—in medical terms—to expect me to be a drooling zombie for the rest of my life. Somehow, and someday, I may know how the sun broke through the dark clouds over my mind. I knew that Jesus saved me. He heard my heart cry when facing death by demons trying to imprison me in my own mind. His Word spoke to me, for "The secret things belong to the Lord our God, but the things revealed belong to us and to our children forever." Deuteronomy 29:29. I learned that I'm not meant to know the secret things, for "Who has known the mind of the Lord so as to instruct him? But we have the mind of Christ." 1 Corinthians 2:16. I believe what happened was real and surreal.

I met the African Princess soon after my revelation, and she explained that she attempted suicide after her fiancé jilted her at the altar and that I was his doppelganger. When she saw me, she thought I was the devil. I blessed her with the truth of salvation through Christ and taught her that the devil was a liar. And God revealed to me how Dr. R. had tricked me with the loud music and the floating smoke rings so I wouldn't see him blowing the small pill across the table with his breath, because all I saw was the pill rolling toward me. I turned nineteen in South Oaks and was released soon after my birthday, in early October, when the leaves started to change. A supercharged Jesus Freak for real, but like an infant lost in the wilderness, I didn't know shit. I just knew that Jesus delivered me from South Oaks, that I was saved by his blood, and that my family and friends were not ready for my radical awakening.

Doubt, a powerful tool of the devil, never leaves us. It lingers, waiting for the right moment to pounce. Twenty years later while driving home from work in Bridgeport, Connecticut, I started thinking about South Oaks and my life since then. I thought about the battle over my soul in the room that morning. I imagined the staff might've attributed the scratches on the wall to me, but had I caused that damage, my nails would have been broken or ground down to the tips of my bloody fingers, leaving a red trail of scratches in that cement wall, a specific trajectory from bed to bed. So I pondered and questioned the reality of that moment in my life. I had taken a ton of drugs and almost drank myself to death. I danced the Thorazine Shuffle while hospitalized. Did it really happen as I remembered, or was it all a long, hallucinatory season in the life of a dual diagnosis, manic depressive with schizoid features? I called my sister, curious what memories she kept, and God baptized me in the Holy Spirit when she said, "Oh yeah, I remember seeing those scratches on the wall."

"On Becoming Christ"

You lived the signs:
Loved horror movies
At an early age,
Read all that was written on the occult,
Carried on telepathic romances
With young impressionable girls,
Meditated on the Moon.
You even experienced some
Modest psychokinetic success,
Witnessed by a chosen few.

You fell out of body
cruised the ceiling,
watching T.V. in the new cellular light.
And there were substances necessary
for stimulation beyond that of mortal man.

Some said you opened the door
to evil perception, the foulness.
But the crowbar felt cold and right in your hand
as you walked the streets
a possessed soldier of speed.

TIME announced the coming of the child
in the tube, the real Frankenstein's monster
revealed with the true prophecy,
anti-Christ, your brother,
defeated by one of his own
you the secret agent assassin obscene,
cunning in violence and lies.

While the Christian world waited
for the sky trumpet to sound off in triumph,
you'd slip through the shadows
and drive his black heart back to hell
forever, freeing all to receive
the power of the New Word.

Fuck the fallen angels
disguised in their white jackets
and smiles as they suck

you into vials to measure
the Lithium in your blood.

They cannot stop you.
you eat their souls
with Thorazine for breakfast.

"For we wrestle not against flesh and blood but against principalities,
against powers, against the rulers of the darkness of this world, against
spiritual wickedness in the high places. Wherefore take unto you the
whole armor of God, that ye may withstand in the evil day, and having
done all, to stand."

EPHESIANS 6: 12,13

20

JESUS IS JUST ALRIGHT WITH ME

I WAS BACK IN TOWN—A TRUE BORN-AGAIN JESUS FREAK—WEAR-
ing all the bells and whistles. I heard the calling of an evangelist
the moment I emerged from the comatose room. I only wanted
to tell everyone about Jesus and thought I only needed to share
my South Oaks testimony, and people would instantly fall to their
knees crying out for the Lord, like I cried out when the demons
pinned my arm. I wore a massive wooden cross around my neck,
pinned a couple of big Jesus buttons on my jacket and carried a
pocket full of Bible tracts I received from a guy I met at the mall
named Adam. He asked me what church I attended. Having been
raised a traditional tortured Catholic, I wanted nothing to do with
a church but agreed to accompany the guy to a worship service the
following Sunday. He picked me up in his lime-green Gremlin and
drove us to his pastor Bob's house. His house? They set up chairs in
a two-car garage where about twenty members sat in attendance,
mostly yuppies. I never attended a church service like this but
started to move in the flow, singing traditional hymns. When Pastor Bob preached it sounded good. He didn't just read verses from
the mass manual followed by everyone reading a response in that
dull, monotone robotic voice. He actually talked about Jesus and
recited verses from memory. I didn't know about the accuracy, but

I guessed I could look them up to verify; in fact I could do it during the sermon because they gave me a New King James Bible as a gift, which made me wonder what was wrong with the old King James. And he quoted the verses with power and passion each time, like in 2 Timothy 1: 7, which says that "For God has not given us a spirit of fear, but of power and of love and of a sound mind." That excited me, because I learned the truth at South Oaks. I wanted to share my testimony and started feeling the love until I spoke with Pastor Bob, and he told me that the world was going to end in three years so we needed to get ready, and God gave him the gift of healing, and he healed himself of cancer by reaching into his body, cutting through his flesh using his own hand, and pulling out the tumor from his lungs. It didn't sound like he was operating with a sound mind to me, and I quickly got out of there.

Back in town, partying and praising the Lord, I looked scarier than ever. Unlike Jesus, who left Nazareth to begin his ministry, my mission started at home. I gathered my family around the kitchen table. I told them that all I needed was Jesus, how I could be left in the middle of the wilderness, without anything, no survival skills, not even a match, and Jesus would provide; that if he called me to walk out into traffic, he would protect me, so that by this miracle others would come to believe. They sat speechless, looking around at each other. I could see their fear and disbelief. I expected this response, because I read about when Jesus returned home to Nazareth, the people rejected him and plotted to kill him. I knew my family wasn't plotting to kill me. I wasn't Jesus, but if I prayed for their salvation in faith, God would make a way for them to stand up from under their sins.

Free from the cloud of deception, but brainwashed by the neuroscience, I bought into the lie that I needed to take Lithium for the rest of my life and figured I'd make the best of it. I also started seeing a local psychologist, Dr. K., a plump, thirty-something Jewish man with a receding hairline. I never asked him about it, but I guess he wore his yarmulke during our sessions because he saw me after teaching Torah to his son. It didn't bother me. Jesus was a Jew, and I asked God if he planned for me to lead Dr. K.

into his kingdom; I'd read about Messianic Jews. But we didn't talk about God. I trusted Dr. K. He sincerely cared. I trusted him, and we spent most of the time talking about masturbation and being released from my guilt. It felt good to talk about it.

"I gave you milk, not solid food, for you were not ready for it. Indeed, you are still not ready."

1 CORINTHIANS 3:2

21

DEPRESSION

Deep depression buried me alive. I wrote down a verse I liked that crazy Pastor Bob quoted: "Be sober, be vigilant for your adversary, the devil, as a roaring lion walketh about, seeking whom he may devour." 1 Peter 5:8. I decided to go off the Lithium and receive God's healing, and the black hole of depression became the roaring lion. I knew I needed to keep moving, so I found a job driving and delivering paper goods all over Long Island. I got there at 6:00 a.m. on my first day, loaded the van and took the list of business addresses and the big Thomas Guides Map of Long Island. I made the first couple of local deliveries in Huntington, then became lost in a maze of the Northern State, Southern State Parkways, the Sunrise Highway, Robert Moses Parkway, 25, 25A, finding nothing, becoming angry, frustrated, and scared when I drove onto the Long Island Expressway. The sun sinking into night and making only two out of twenty deliveries sank my mind further into despair. Almost ready to let go, I closed my eyes, released the steering wheel doing 65 miles per hour and counted to five. I opened my eyes and grabbed the wheel. I risked crashing, maybe killing myself and other drivers, but God saved me; I closed my eyes again, let go and counted to ten, opened my eyes, grabbed the wheel, saved again, this time in the middle lane! Sweating and my heart racing, I closed my eyes for the third time, let go and counted to fifteen. People started honking their horns all around me; I opened my eyes and became blinded by the bright lights in the rearview mirror. I grabbed the wheel, stiff armed, locked out and almost fishtailed into the right and left lanes. Three was a holy number, so I stopped and found my way back to the paper company. The pissed-off manager fired me on the spot, yelling about the money I caused the company to lose. I walked out of the warehouse and slumped down on the curb, waiting for Mom to come and pick me up. As we drove home, I told her what happened, not the closed eyes driving, just my complete and total failure to do the job.

I shrunk further into the black hole and started believing the enemy's lies: I was alone, and the Lord abandoned me because I actually attempted suicide and homicide! I tempted God. Alone again, the demons returned to me, and all I could do was sleep and eat. I'd wake each day, later into the afternoon and do nothing but watch T.V. and eat. Time unfolded into the timeless space. Each day, I felt more exhausted. My muscles turned into fat. I went to bed at three in the morning and woke at three in the afternoon. I couldn't hear what my mom and sister were saying to me. But Mom never gave up. Before leaving for work, she'd come into my room, pull my blanket off and pull me halfway out of bed by grabbing my ankles. "Raymond! You have to get up!"

I went to sleep at night hoping to never wake up. Living in Tito's old room isolated me at the far end of the house. I loved his old Motorola turntable, centered in a stained wood cabinet with speakers on each side and slots on top for record albums. The radio worked. But I didn't turn it on that morning when I laid down on the bed and pulled the blanket over my body . . . hopefully for the last time. Restless, wrestling in prayer, doubting my faith, I finally fell asleep, then awoke to Spanish music playing on the radio and someone trying to pull my blanket off. I pulled back into a tug-of-war with a dark silhouette at the side of my bed. The tension in the blanket increased, and time folded into dawn in a blink of an eye. I didn't want to let go. Then a sunbeam shined on the stranger, revealing his slick black hair, dark eyes, high cheekbones, white shirt, necktie, and light beige suit. I didn't want to let go. I didn't want to get up. I wanted to pull the blanket over my head and hide. And die. But he pulled more forcefully, and I felt my grip weakening and my fingers slipping as he ripped the blanket from my hands. I sat up; the Spanish music played, but the room was empty, and the sunbeams caught dust in their light—floating in the music—while the blanket lay on the other side of the room under the Motorola.

The clock read 6:00 a.m. Everyone still slept. The house stayed silent, but I heard the birds singing outside. I stood up and walked out into the dining room. My mind started clearing out space for a sense of perception, the sense of knowing what happened and why. I stopped at the dining room table and saw the old photo album that Mom went through after Tito died, still laying there, months later. I opened it and turned the pages until I found him sitting there in an old photo I'd never seen, wearing the same light suit, the same white shirt with a necktie, high cheekbones, dark eyes, and slick black hair. Only in the photo, Tito smiled.

I guess that's where Mom picked it up, that "morning wake-up blanket pull technique." She learned it from Tito and added the ankle-pull finish. And so I now had two people telling me to get up: my mom, before leaving for the graveyard shift, and Tito, coming back from the grave. I got up the next morning at six and figured getting back in shape to be a good place to start. Now thirty pounds overweight with bad skin, I used to be a beast before South Oaks. I could always pump out the push-ups; after the *Rocky* movie, I started drinking raw eggs and doing one-arm push-ups, working up to fifty with each arm and one hundred with both. I got down, started doing two-arm push-ups and collapsed onto my face at fifty-four, good enough for the first day. Depressed by my weakness, I pushed on to the Bible. I wanted to experience The Living Word I heard so much about, not just words telling a story. I picked up my Bible and decided to call God out—I mean call out to God—by tossing it onto the table, saying "Alright God, speak to me." I looked down and saw the book opened to Isaiah 54. I got excited about that. Maybe the truth could be found in the numbers. I started reading about barren women singing for joy, clearly not for me, but I kept going and read, "For a small moment have I forsaken thee, but with great mercies will I gather thee. In a little wrath, I hid my face from thee for a moment but with everlasting kindness will I have mercy on thee sayeth the Lord thy redeemer." Isaiah 54: 7, 8

I stopped and read the words again, and again, and again, until the rest of the words became a blur and those verses became clear, like light, and God knew not only my heart for Christ, but also the questions in my mind about why I suffered for so long. He answered me in spite of myself, my judgment about the meaning of his instruction. He was saying stop, right now, this moment, and hear; what's nineteen years in the fold of unfolding time? Not even a blink of an eye, not even a full breath. And I received it in my heart, chiseled in my mind, and I knew he wrote it for me in the space of a small moment, through a prophet who lived long ago; I knew there would be more words, and words, and words, written not on tablets of stone, but on the tablet of my heart, forever blazing in my mind, waiting to be spoken into the next small moment.

I read about Jesus hanging out with tax collectors and sinners and thought it was cool, a natural way for me to share my testimony and spread The Word where I did a lot of sinning. I also needed to work, so I started bouncing again, this time closer to home at the Abby Tavern, a small pub in Commack off of Jericho Turnpike. Steve DeLuca brought me in. I met Steve after I was released from South Oaks. He was dating my next-door neighbor, Laura St. Pierre, and was friends with Laura's older brother, Vinny. I was very close to both of them. Steve's a few years older than me, and played football at South. He was thickly muscled, barrel chested, and had huge biceps. He was also intelligent and level headed. He became like my older brother. Steve worked the front door and I covered the back. Mom was angry with him for getting me the job. He told her he was trying to help and that sometimes it worked out when you made the gunslinger the sheriff. She still wasn't happy but Dad thanked Steve for being a good friend. The bartender, a Vietnam Vet named Rick, came out of Nam with wild eyes. I knew he saw unspeakable things over there, because he never spoke about it and people didn't ask because they didn't want to know. But I wanted to know about Vietnam, and I wanted to be there when Rick was ready to tell his history. The Tavern was another spot where people pre-partied before going out to the big clubs, like Good Times, in the same shopping center and featuring the best club bands on Long Island. Occasionally they had a big-name rocker. The Tavern offered the usual: pool table, foosball table, jukebox, darts, and booths where folks munched down from a simple menu of burgers and fries. I was a good bouncer, in your face if needed—and fast—but also kind and considerate to deserving souls.

I expected to be tested by people I knew, some who knew my story and wanted to see the Jesus Freak in action. One night, a group of ex-basketball jocks from North sat in a booth waiting for their food. Their leader, Mark G., lit up a joint. Mark, an accomplished athlete, stood 6'5" played center and could also fight. His rep as a tough guy came from beating up a couple of greasers. I told him to give me the joint or I'd make him eat it. He washed it down with a beer. Hallelujah. I just wanted to love people, but I could still feel that force of fear, drawing me in, feeding my anger. One night, a guy from King's Park squared off to fight a local. I came up from behind, got him in a rear naked chokehold and took him straight down. He hit the back of his head hard off the floor and went from stupid drunk to dazed and confused. I requested that he and his friends leave the premises, and they fortunately complied. I'm sure my takedown impressed them, and they felt further motivated by the gathering of locals standing behind me. Steve became the manager of Good Times and brought me with him. He also trained as a bodybuilder and we started working out together. We became brothers in iron.

We started training every day, living healthy (at least during the day for me, a new experience) and taking protein supplements, including my favorite, desiccated Argentinian beef liver tablets. We ate about thirty a day, and when the time came to squat, people knew to get away from the racks. I dropped down to my fighting weight of 200 pounds, making me the smallest guy on the Good Times crew. Pat H., a local legend tough guy, worked the front door. Pat, 6'4" and 240 pounds of ripped muscle and full sleeves, was a boilermaker by trade, a biker by night, and a trainer of German Shepard police dogs on the side. The cops often brought their wanna-be criminals around, as part of their "reprimand and release" program, to participate in Pat's physical counseling program around the back of the club. He never told us the amount of gratuity he received, and no one had the balls to ask. Kevin, the other bouncer at the door, carried a similar frame but looked very conservative, like Clark Kent, with his short black hair and black-rimmed glasses. He could bench 500 pounds and would just pick guys up and take them out of the club in a fireman's carry when necessary. I worked the stage, usually positioned to the left side in front of these eight-foot speakers. All the other bouncers wore earplugs for protection, a smart move because the music was super loud. But I didn't think it cool to have to pull plugs out of my ears to talk to the young ladies. So I now have fifty-percent hearing loss in my right ear. A couple of big names played the club, like Rick Derringer, and Leslie West and Mountain, but the regular shows were top club bands like Zebra and Twisted Sister. Both bands eventually outgrew the smaller clubs and ended up signing record contracts, going on concert tours and making videos for MTV. The guys in Twisted Sister pushed the envelope. Dee Synder and the other band members usually played their sets in speedos. Dee offered me a job as a roadie, but I declined. I suppose my life might have turned out markedly different had I accepted. Good Times, frequented by people from North, South, and Kings Park, provided another place for fighting, especially on Saturday nights. Our job as bouncers required moving the combatants out the door and off the sidewalk in front of the club. What they did in the parking lot provided great entertainment; sometimes we'd watch idiots pounding each other's faces into the pavement. From idiot to observer of idiots. North and South had established somewhat of a truce, but Kings Park people always showed up on the warpath.

Those foolish enough to be on their side of the tracks, alone or in small groups, risked getting the shit beat out them, serious injury and hospitalization. It got so bad at one point that we refused to admit anyone into the club with an ID or driver's license showing a Kings Park address.

The Lopez home sat around the corner from the Larkfield Pub, about fifty yards as the crow flies from our front door. The bar, also known as The Twilight Zone, changed many times over the years, from an old man's watering hole to a biker bar to our place—the launching and landing zone for our frequent journeys into night. It included the usual pool table, foosball table, dartboard and a place for business transactions. Brian B. sold speed and weed, and we worked out a mutually beneficial arrangement. I provided security for his drug deals in exchange for Black Beauties or 697s. He also set up arm-wrestling matches in the pub, taking five-dollar bets; I usually won, which worked fine unless people refused to pay. Then there'd be a fight. The losers, always visitors and not regulars, didn't know any better.

"The Twilight Zone"
(Tribute to Frankie Cocaine)

We were cool playing pool
   in the Twilight Zone.
We knew all 'bout 8 ball,
   green slate I would own.
Drinking beer with no fear
   gulping down white speed.
Acting tough, talking rough,
   making knuckles bleed.
There were dudes doing ludes
   falling through the glass.
Others stood (if they could)
   smoking Jamaican grass.
We would fight. I would bite
   in the Twilight Zone.
Showing might in the night
   that was all we'd known.

In the day we would pay
                with our pounding brains.
Like a jerk, go to work
                drugs still in our veins.
Come real soon, afternoon
                we would crawl back in.
Breathe stale smoke, cough and choke,
                Sip on watered gin.
Then we'd wait in our hate
                for the evening meal:
Frank Cocaine in his pain,
                so stoned he would kneel,
On the floor by the door,
                straining to get out.
First he cried, then he died
                all of us did shout:
We are cool playing pool
                in the Twilight Zone!
Our disease, lost the keys
                no way to get home . . .
Damn our hex, easy sex
                this would fool us too.
With a bitch or a witch
                trapped inside the zoo.
In the stench we would wrench
                feeling all alone
And we'd cry, and we'd lie
                and tell you we had grown.
With a punch in the gut
                you could hear us moan:
If we try we can die
                in the Twilight Zone.

Frankie overdosed on heroin and was found dead one morning, sitting in his car in front of the bar with a needle in his arm. We all attended his funeral service, where we met his mother and brother. We never knew he had a family.

My final battle with John D. took place at the Twilight Zone. He owned a landscaping business, basically a one-truck operation with a couple of workers. He also drove Upstate in the winter to cut firewood. There were a handful of guys shooting up heroin then, and John was one of them. Always an asshole, he took it to a new level on a landscaping job for Mrs. B. The B family belonged to the original hootenanny partiers and were longtime neighborhood friends. Fran and I spent years playing soldiers and baseball together when we were young, but for some reason I never understood, he became a huge KISS fan. I loved the family and felt sad for them after Mr. B. died from cancer when we were kids. John worked high on dope most of the time, and one day Mrs. B. told him that she no longer needed his services. He responded by terrorizing her. He stormed into her home and emptied several bags of fertilizer throughout her house before he left. Around the same time, he also beat the shit out of a local guy, George, whom he outweighed by 100 pounds. John weighed about 250. He went after George because he went out with John's girlfriend. A lot of people knew that the girl pursued George. John came into the Twilight Zone one night and started pounding down shots at the bar. The sight of him started brewing the rage in my gut. I got all worked up and finally walked up and stood behind him. He could see me in the mirror behind the bar, and we just stood there for a while. He kept drinking, and I kept staring at the back of his head, imagining what I was going to do to him, until he turned around and asked, "What's your beef?" to which I responded, "This is my beef," and commenced reigning rapid-fire lefts and rights to his head. He went out on his feet, but the bar kept him upright; I kept wailing on him until I gassed out and he went down. We were both nineteen, and this was my last fight. A few years later, John died from an overdose, and I felt a sense of peace for both of us.

The Twilight Zone could be a dangerous place, and many times I received mercy. We got along with folks from Elwood, just west of Commack, and they also partied in The Zone. Michael H. from Elwood sold weed there, had a black belt in Tae Kwan Do, and could knock a guy out with one punch. I saw him do it. My sister also sold a little weed, creating a possible risk of some competitive conflict at the Zone. One night while dominating the pool table, I looked up just in time to see Michael H. and my sister arguing just outside the front door. I then saw him throw a violent sidekick into Craig's chest, launching him across the hood of a car, after he stepped in to intervene on my sister's behalf. This was quite the heroic act by Craig, as he was a lover, not a fighter. But sometimes you have to fight for what you love. Teresa and Craig would get married twenty years later. Who knew? They certainly didn't know at the time. The exact circumstances aren't all that important, but I learned that Michael said a few unkind words to my sister. I couldn't let that be. I walked into the pub and saw him at the back, leaning against a cabinet, waiting to play pool. I walked up to him, placed my hands on the countertop, pinning him into the corner, and said, "Mike, you need to apologize to my sister." He agreed and apologized right then and there. Thank you, Jesus.

The photo I found of my grandfather after his ghost pulled the blanket off my bed.

"For the word of God is alive and active. Sharper than any double-edged sword, it penetrates even to dividing soul and spirit, joints and marrow; it judges the thoughts and attitudes of the heart."

HEBREWS 4:12

22

THE BIG JEWELRY STORE JOB

I DON'T REMEMBER BEING AT PEOPLE'S PUB THAT NIGHT, BUT I DO remember getting shitfaced drunk and taking a Quaalude with Eddie. I also remember the two of us walking down the sidewalk along the stores of a strip mall and coming across a brick or a stone (I don't know and I don't remember) that just happened to be laying in front of a jewelry store, as if someone left it there for us to use; throwing it through the display window seemed like a good idea at the time, and Eddie grabbed all the precious jewelry and stuffed it in his pockets. I don't remember how we got to my house, but my sister recalled that I called her and asked her to come pick us up. My friends from the Second Precinct were there waiting for us, and we persuaded her to keep driving. When they pulled us over, they found all the jewelry in the back seat where Eddie dumped it. They were going to arrest all three of us, and we told them Teresa had nothing to do with it, so she didn't get arrested . . . and that was good.

"For I have the desire to do what is good, but I cannot carry it out. For I do not do the good I want to do, but the evil I do not want to do—this I keep on doing."

ROMANS 7: 18,19

23

JAIL TIME

We spent the morning at the Second Precinct lockup; then they took us to court in Hauppauge for arraignments. Eddie already served six months at Riverhead and faced some serious time Upstate if he caught another felony conviction. So out of the deepest love and loyalty, I decided to exonerate him and take the entire rap. My sister told Mom about our arrest, and as usual, Mom came to court. We enjoyed a Hooligan reunion in lockup; Brian R. presented for some kind of pretrial hearing on his robbery case, and Lloyd got arraigned on a burglary charge. We were all appearing before Judge Ohlig. I had appeared before him twice previously. When they called my name, I stood up tall and told the judge that I committed the crime, and Eddie had nothing to do with it, much to the dismay of the public defender handling the arraignments that day. The judge told me to shut up and acknowledge that I understood the charge against me, Third Degree Burglary, and then do what my attorney advised me to do. I pled not guilty, and a discussion on bail ensued. The judge knew my mom from the ER as a former patient. The following exchange then took place: "Mrs. Lopez, I'm sorry to see you here again under these circumstances, but it looks like some reasonable bail conditions can be arranged.

Please talk to your son's attorney and I'll recall Raymond's case when you are ready."

"I can't do it anymore your honor." I couldn't believe the words I was hearing. Mom always bailed me out. Sure, she'd let me stay overnight in the precinct lockup, but this was county jail! "What's that, Mrs. Lopez?" "I can't keep doing this your honor. He's not changing. I don't know what else to do and I just can't . . ." "That's alright, Mrs. Lopez, we have a place where your son can go, and perhaps he'll learn something while he's there. Remanded to Riverhead County Jail. Counsel motions are due within two weeks of today."

Shackled to the chain gang, waists and ankles, we enjoyed a good time on the bus ride east, acting badass, like we didn't care. But then we arrived. I had never been to county jail, not even to visit. Stripped down naked, they threw some white powdery shit all over me, to kill any lice, then sprayed me down using something like a mini fire hose that hurt. Then squat down, deep, spread your cheeks and cough, spread em' again and cough, louder this time! Then back in the same clothes and separated and taken to different tiers. I was nineteen. Most of the guys on my tier were black dudes, and a couple of Puerto Ricans, all in their twenties and thirties, maybe older. The tier consisted of individual cells, and tables and benches welded to the bars, spread evenly so four guys could sit to eat their meals, play cards, or just bullshit. Kitchen trustees slid food served on plastic plates, along with plastic forks and knives, through slots in the bars at each table, while the supervising CO counted every item passed in and out before ordering the trustees to take the carts away. Most of the guys came from Brentwood and Central Islip, and the guy in the cell to my left never shut up. He wore some kind of silky shirt and tight pants with slight bellbottoms, like he had been arrested at the disco. He talked up a storm, and so fast, most of the time that I didn't even know what he was saying. He called me "Lopes" and kept me up most nights. I felt scared and always kept my back to the bars. And I kept pounding out those one-arm push-ups, like Rocky. I worked back up to doing fifty with each arm and did different variations of push-ups throughout the day. I told everyone that I needed to stay in shape because I received a scholarship to play football at San Diego State. The three or four shower stalls at the end of the tier, near the COs' station, smelled foul. I didn't shower. I called my sister collect every day to ask her to bail me out. She said she didn't have the money, but I knew Mom told her to let me stay in for a while. One night, my manic neighbor told me he overheard the COs talking about a pervert who got gangbanged on another tier. I had a nightmare that night.

"The Rape"

Grease coverin' my skin
so thick that I play
tic-tac-toe on my forearm
carvin' Xs and Os with my fingernails.
But I'm not steppin' in that sump of a shower again.
The last time I was in there my feet
sank up to my ankles in some breathin' brown shit.
There's no rule that ya have to shower in here.
They won't waste water hosin' ya down.

This is a main black tier,
twenty three bloods and all crazy niggers.
Then there's my big brown ass and some skinny Gabacho.

I just can't believe they put him in here.
I heard a rumor runnin' through the blood
that he was a chester molester.
The guards started it.
He was the tier punchin' bag. In fact
you couldn't even call him white anymore.
He was a permanent black and blue.

The air was racin' through the bars
that day. There was a hunger hangin' in the cells.
At the end of the tier were sittin'six whisperin' wolves.
The Gabacho was leanin' on the bars
with his elbows, and his hands hangin' down.
They all kept starin' at him hard.
Then they came; they picked him up,
shoved a dirty sock in his mouth,

and carried him like a floppin' fish out of water
to the last cell farthest down.
Everyone disappeared in the shadows
and the tier got empty,
then filled with
one long cry
like a tortured dog howlin' through a muzzle.
It got so loud I couldn't hear
my own fear.
It was a sicknin' kind of fear
that went through me fast.
My body was tremblin'
drivin' my knees into the floor
I crawled into my cell
and got to be part of the plumbin' under the sink.
I tried to push myself through the wall
then it was like his throat caved in,
his voice suddenly choked off.
And I could hear them;
moanin' and groanin' and moanin' and groanin'
and the sound of their sweaty thighs
slappin' and slappin' and slappin'!

Later,
they came
and carried him away on a stretcher.
He was all curled in a ball
and shakin' like he was freezin' cold.
There was dried blood caked in cracked clumps
all over his back and his ass
and he was still bleedin'!
His blood soaked through the stretcher
and was drippin' from underneath
a thin red trial.

So now, the bars rub sores on my back
but I won't sit any other way.
All I do is play tic-tac-toe
carvin' Xs and Os
X-O, X-O, X-O. . .

I don't know how long I stayed in jail after my arrest on January 25, 1979. My sister said a few days, so let's call it a week. It was my awakening. I knew I could never go back, but I didn't know what to do. I had no plan. On May 11, 1979, I pled guilty to Petit Larceny, a Class A misdemeanor, and the good Judge Ohlig sentenced me to three years' probation. My probation officer, Mr. Roselloe, turned out to be a good guy. He'd come to the house and we'd have coffee. I'd go to his office to drop a urine sample and a paycheck stub. I knew he held the power to send me back to Riverhead, but I also new that he cared about me, and that was cool. I thought being a probation officer was a good job, maybe something I could do someday.

"Suddenly an angel of the Lord appeared and a light shone in the cell. He struck Peter on the side and woke him up. 'Quick get up!' he said and the chains fell off Peter's wrists . . . Peter followed him out of the prison . . ."

ACTS 12: 7–9

24

ANSWERED PRAYER

MY SISTER AND HER FRIENDS MOVED TO CALIFORNIA IN JUNE
1979. They drove in two vans and caravanned across the country,
a very cool adventure. Two days prior to her departure, Mom told
Teresa she was having an affair with a soccer dad she spent time
with on a trip to Germany with my youngest brother's team. My
parents hadn't communicated effectively for twenty years. The day
before she left, Mom took Teresa to have lunch with this guy, and
all he did was talk about himself. After Teresa left for California,
the holy shit hit the fan. Mom and this guy decided to tell their
spouses that they wanted a divorce and planned on marrying. The
spouses did not take it well. The guy's wife locked herself in a bathroom and slit her wrists. Thank God she survived. They had young
children. Dad hit mom and went on a drinking binge. I don't know
where they went, but my mom and brothers left the house and
stayed away for I don't know how long. I stayed home with Dad,
and we drank together, shots of whiskey, starting around noon.
And for Dad, everything was crap, every day, every moment spent,
worth nothing at all. Now, I could drink better than the best of
them, but this kind of angry, suffering drinking became too much
for me. We drank for about a week, and when I tried to take the
bottle away, Dad grabbed my wrist and just glared at me; I decided

it wasn't a good idea. He eventually sobered up, and my mom and brothers came back home. My parents decided to end their marriage. Dad came into my room one evening and told me that they made a dinner reservation and were going out for the last time to discuss the separation and divorce. He told me everything would be okay, but I could see the sad desperation in his eyes. I decided to pray. I found a great photo in the dining room of my parents on a boat. They looked so happy. My mother was gorgeous. She always wore her hair short. They were smiling, happy. Their eyes were sparkling. I brought the photo into my room, knelt down before it, and prayed that the love displayed would get them through. I held the framed photo and meditated on the love between them. They came home after a couple of hours. Dad walked into my room for a second time that night and said, "I don't know how to explain it, but we're going to be alright. We're going to stay together and work it out." I didn't need an explanation.

The photo I meditated on when I prayed for my parents.

"Therefore I tell you, whatever you ask for in prayer, believe that you have received it, and it will be yours."

MARK 11:24

25

MERCY

I NEEDED MONEY SO I WENT BACK TO BOUNCING AT GOOD TIMES.
Mom wasn't happy. It was the same song and dance, Bible in one
hand, door in the other, trying to save wayward souls, particularly
the young ladies. It was a dangerous place on many levels. One
Sunday morning after closing, around 4:00 a.m., a private party
broke out for Pat and his dog-training buddies. I took a Quaalude
that night—always a mistake—because every time I took one, I
got arrested. But on this day, the dawn of a new day of mercy in
spite of my sins, things ended differently. A huge fight erupted,
loud enough to draw the attention of the proprietors of the Jewish
deli next door. The fight was a total blackout for me. I suddenly
found myself hiding in the bathroom with two bartenders and
one of the other bouncers. I lost my shirt, and my knuckles were
bloody and swollen. We could hear the cops in the club shouting
out commands, "Get down! Put your hands behind your back!"
and arresting people. Shit! I'm on probation, and if I get arrested,
I'm done. Out of nowhere, someone handed me a horrible plaid
sports jacket and the Sunday edition of *Newsday*. Brilliant! I'll just
walk out of the bathroom and stroll through the club, right past
the cops. Good morning, officers. I was just out for my morning
stroll to get the paper. Beautiful morning isn't it? No need for a

shirt, but a jacket is mandatory on a Sunday morning. I heard this racket inside and thought I'd enter to see if I could help. Right!? And, that's exactly what happened. I walked straight out, right past the cops, without uttering a word. It wasn't Jedi mind control. It was a miracle.

I needed to get out of Commack, and God provided a way. I worked as a counselor one summer at a Fresh Air Fund camp in Fishkill, New York. The director was running another camp and contacted me to see if I wanted to work as an assistant cook. It provided a perfect escape, a way to make some money and enjoy some fresh air on the Appalachian Trail. They decided to throw a going-away party for me at Good Times. I didn't have a car at the time and got around on my Raleigh ten speed that Dad bought me years before, to try to get me into competitive cycling. I rode the five miles from my house to Good Times, and after drinking all night, I attempted to ride home.

I woke up that Sunday morning lying in a ten-foot ditch alongside Indian Head Road, a dangerous stretch between Commack and Kings Park, where many accidents took place. I opened my eyes, only to be blinded by the sun. My brain felt like a bass drum being pounded on both sides. The paralyzing horror—the horror, the horror that seized me after I woke up on my back in the dirt and garbage—lasted for a small moment, then vanished like a vapor by the time I stood up and dusted the dirt away. I climbed up out of the ditch and over the metal railing to find my bike missing. I hitched a ride home and packed my bags.

When I got back at the end of the summer, I found a job as a counselor at St. Mary of the Angel's Home, a group home in Syosset for boys on PINS (Persons in Need of Supervision) petitions, who were wards of the court. Most of the kids came from Brooklyn and The Bronx, ranging in ages from thirteen to eighteen. Craig drove me to the interview and lit up a joint on the way, so I could be relaxed during the interview. I brought my camp counselor experience that I could elaborate on, and I felt very relaxed. I got the job, mercy, mercy me, and I was on my way.

Along the way, I started feeling so good about myself that I blew off Mr. Roselloe. I missed a few appointments but called and left messages apologizing and explaining how busy I was and how well things were going. I received a few appointment letters from Roselloe, but I didn't worry about it. I was working, having an impact on young lives, and only drinking and smoking weed.

About four months went by before I finally reported to Roselloe. One Saturday morning the phone rang, and I picked up. There were no answering machines or caller ID, so you picked up to see who was calling. It was Roselloe, and he simply said, "Get your ass down to my office. Now." Then he hung up. Click. Dad allowed me to use the Dodge Dart since I started working again. Roselloe knew it took twenty minutes to drive to his office. I got there and waited for an hour before he brought me in. "Do you know how many people I have on my caseload?" "Uh, I don't know, fifty?" "Try 250. I can't waste my time. I have a system. When you miss three scheduled office visits, you have chronically failed to report as instructed; I get a warrant for your arrest, your probation is revoked and you go back to Riverhead for a year." He showed me the warrant application on his desk. He held up his pen and said, "I was about to sign it and walk it over the clerk's office, and for some reason, I have no idea why, I decided to give you a call. If you hadn't picked up, the warrant would be signed, and you'd be on your way to county jail. So I'm going to hold off." He picked up the warrant and showed me. "You see I've left this space blank for including a second violation." He handed me the little plastic bottle and said, "You're going to give me a urine sample right now, and if it's dirty, you're going away." I thought shit, I've been smoking weed every day, God Almighty! Please Lord, let me give a clean UA. I gave Roselloe the sample, and he gave me an appointment to come in the following week. No way I wasn't going to show. I had to be prepared to go, so I got my sister to drive me. It wasn't the parting of the Red Sea, but the UA came back clean. And so it goes.

"Praise be to the Lord, for he has heard my cry for mercy."

PSALMS 28:6

26

RUNNING INTO PAULA

PAULA AND I ENJOYED A NUMBER OF RENDEZVOUS OVER THE years, never consummated, never followed up with a phone call or visit the next day. But one romantic evening, that all changed. The Whistle Stop in Smithtown was just another place people went to party. It had live music, and of course, a foosball table. There were two floors, maybe three, and I was running up the stairs from the bottom level when we ran into each other as she was racing down to play foosball with her girlfriends. We've been together ever since that small moment, and so it goes. It became so much more than what it had always been for me: her green eyes, blonde hair, great body, and the smell of patchouli. She was simply the kindest, most loving, and smartest person. And she thought she was funny, which was funny. We came together. My parents loved her. Her friends thought she was crazy, or at the very least, didn't know what she was doing.

Paula had plans. She worked as a waitress since the age of sixteen and went to college, even though she changed her major three times (and would change it another three times before finally earning her PhD fifteen years later). She also earned a second-degree brown belt in Isshin-Ryu karate, and she could kick ass. As a cheerleader and sprinter in high school, she had very strong legs.

We enjoyed play fighting together, and one night after drinking too much wine, she nailed me with a perfect spinning roundhouse kick to the sternum as I charged in to take her down. My shoulders hit the ground first, and the bruise to my sternum turned a deep purple.

On another warm night in June 1980, we sat in my parents' backyard alongside the pool. Paula told me about her decision to move to Los Angeles to live with her friend, Melanie, work as a waitress, go to community college for free, and pick up some of the general ed courses she needed to graduate. I instantly made one of the many fateful command decisions in my life and proposed that we go together and move in with my sister and her boyfriend. I had been talking to Teresa for roughly a year about moving to California. Her boyfriend's father was a licensed contractor, and there was a job waiting for me. It was all set. We agreed to move to California and live with my sister and her boyfriend until we got a place of our own! It was about three months before my twenty-first birthday, and my parents fulfilled their commitment to invest in my future by paying for my one-way ticket to LA. I told Roselloe the plan, and he said he'd be happy to put me in for an early termination from probation. I later received a letter from Roselloe, signed by Judge Ohlig, declaring my early termination on September 8, 1980, with a final offering of, "We trust that you have profited from your experience with this department."

"A wife of noble character who can find? She is worth far more than rubies."

PROVERBS 31:10

27

YES

THE DAYS AND WEEKS AND MONTHS RACED BY, AND THINGS
moved along: preparation, plans, and excitement. Paula's parents
showed support, especially her dad, who was very happy for us.
Her mom even took her shopping for luggage, but the day before
we left, she lost it. When Paula went home to pick up her stuff, she
found that her mother had moved every trace of Paula's existence
from her bedroom to the front curb. It would take a year and a
miracle before they spoke again.

The night before we left for California, my parents left me a
note, which a few months before would have been unheard of. The
note told me to invite my friends over for beer and hot dogs for my
twenty-first birthday. And so we partied all night long! Well into
the evening, Padrino, who was staying with us at the time, found
time to steal Paula away. They sat together in the kitchen. He gave
her $300 in cash and instructed, "Do not give this to Raymond."
He then offered her advice in a thick, whiskey-tinged, Cuban accent: "Don't go to California with Raymond. Raymond not right."
Mom walked in at that very moment and told Paula, "Don't listen
to him! He's drunk." She was afraid Paula might decide not to go
and I would follow suit. We all got very drunk that night, which is

perhaps why Mom got lost on the way to JFK that morning, a trip she made hundreds of times; or, she felt sad about us leaving.

We walked through the terminal on our way to the gate and heard Paula's name announced over the loudspeaker, requesting that she report to the customer service desk. We had no idea. Did her mom contact the airline in a desperate act to prevent her from leaving? No. Her Uncle Vinnie upgraded us to first class. The party continued. My sister and her boyfriend planned to welcome us at the gate but didn't show (they were sleeping in their van in the parking lot). LAX is a massive airport, an easy place to get lost, so we went to the baggage claim area, got our bags, and . . .

as we stepped out into the blazing bright California sun of the city of angels I became planted through the concrete deeply rooted in ancestral soil I threw my head back spread my arms wide and breathed in deeply the Holy Spirit sun yes a new son a second life a small moment forever and so it goes yes.